The Interviewer's Book

Hiring the Right Person

Mary Hanson and Brian McIvor

ORPEN PRESS

Published by
Orpen Press
Lonsdale House
Avoca Avenue
Blackrock
Co. Dublin
Ireland

e-mail: info@orpenpress.com
www.orpenpress.com

Paperback ISBN: 978-1-871305-94-4
ePub ISBN: 978-1-909518-13-1
Kindle ISBN: 978-1-909518-14-8

Printed in Ireland by SPRINT-print Ltd.

Acknowledgements

There is a history behind the writing of every book: in this case we, as authors, wished to put down our thoughts and insights on interviewing based on our many years of having worked both separately and together in training, consultancy and managerial roles. We are grateful to our employers, former colleagues and clients, particularly the Irish Management Institute and the Institute of Public Administration, who have provided us with the opportunity to play our part in the drive to develop and improve how organisations and individuals make selection decisions. In particular, we have learned over the years from clients and course participants who have challenged us with real-life situations that they have been faced with. They have forced us to respond with solutions and guidelines that can work in practice, in the real world of selection interviewing. Much of our writing has developed from a distillation of these experiences and interactions.

In our journey to shape these thoughts into a book we received invaluable feedback and advice from the following colleagues: Jack Morrissey, Niall Leavy, Gerry Maloney and Rowan Manihan. We are truly grateful for the time they spent on reading and responding comprehensively to early drafts. We also received very succinct, prompt and expert advice from Mary Redmond on the legal aspects of recruitment and interviewing.

Putting the book into its current shape was also aided hugely by the professional, helpful and friendly assistance of our publishers, in particular our editor, Jennifer Thompson, and also Elizabeth Brennan. It has been a delight to work with them. Thanks must also go to Brian Hallett, for his unfailing eye for style and layout.

Lastly, we would like to thank our families, friends and colleagues who made encouraging noises of support, both when the project was first mooted and during the whole writing process.

Table of Contents

Table of Contents

Table of Contents

Foreword

Any manager who has had to find new employees through an interview process will know just how difficult it can be to make the right choice. There are potential recruits who shine in an interview, but whose performance on the job turns out to be less stellar. Then there are those who struggle to put themselves across well in an interview, but turn out to be ideal employees, motivated and talented. How can you tell who the right person is? There is no magic answer, but the message from this book is that, if the proper preparation is done, then the chances of a successful hire are much higher.

Interviews will never be a perfect process for choosing people – but they are, usually, the best way we have. And making the right choice is so important. For managers and team leaders at all levels, having the right people is vital. A pool of good talent and high performance is the lifeblood of any business, while – as this book underlines – the price of choosing the wrong person is high. In fact, the costs of receiving less than the best performance from employees is immeasurable and can almost always be traced back to poor hiring decisions. Companies spend time and money trying to compensate for gaps in performance but, often, all that is possible is limiting the damage.

The fact that you have bought this book – or are considering doing so – is a sign that, as a potential interviewer, you feel you need some guidance and are prepared to put some time into learning how to conduct the best job search process. This is surely worthwhile. The temptation of busy managers, often not used to interviewing, is to hope that it will all work out and that the best candidate will somehow be clearly evident after a brief, unplanned discussion. If only it was that easy.

Written by experts, this book is an accessible, practical guide, easy to read and full of common sense. It does not contain a magical shortcut to finding the best person. There isn't one. Instead, after underlining that it is really vital to invest time and effort into the recruitment process, it outlines what you need to do at each stage, from searching for candidates, to screening applicants, to the interview process itself. The authors have years of experience, and it shows. They illustrate clearly how the best managers can reap a rich reward from advance thinking and preparation, from careful screening and from a forensic approach to deciding what information they want from candidates and how they will get it, right down to just what questions to ask.

This book addresses the whole recruitment process in a highly practical and accessible way. There is something in it for everyone who ever has to carry out a job interview, whether a seasoned or inexperienced interviewer, from CEO to first-line team leader. It can be dipped into, scanned through, read completely in one sitting or kept as a reference to be used as a refresher before you don the interviewer mantle yet again. You can't afford to make the wrong decision; this book will undoubtedly help you make wiser choices.

Cliff Taylor
Editor, The Sunday Business Post

Preface

Over many years we have been asked into companies of all shapes and sizes to offer practical assistance on aspects of recruitment, selection and performance management. In the process we have seen how managers and team leaders grapple with the business of selection, some with more success than others. We have seen genuine attempts to make the best possible decisions about who is the best person for the job, but we have also seen the other end of the scale, where slipshod practices have been used, generally in an effort to fill a vacancy too quickly. Even in companies where a lot of time and effort is put into the selection process, the best decisions are not always made.

As management consultants, we have worked with many companies on aspects of managing performance at work, and it is in the nature of our business that we are usually asked to work in a remedial context, where someone is not working out well in their job. The investment needed to try to get someone on track and performing adequately can be huge, and the process is not always successful. To us it is clear that these situations often result from a bad hiring decision in the first place.

Over the years we have provided training to many hundreds of interviewers, and in the process we have developed a sense of what does and doesn't work in the selection field. Our clients have valued above all else our use of a practical and relevant approach to interviewing. This book is a distillation of that approach, a pocket guide of sorts, which can be read in one sitting or dipped into as required. It is intended primarily for anyone who has to interview, at any level, and has relevance to both the public and private sectors, and to big and small companies. It will act as a full guide to interviewing for inexperienced interviewers, but also has plenty of useful tips for the practised interviewer who might be forced to rethink some of their techniques after reading it.

We have designed this book with easy reading in mind. It takes the reader from the pre-interview stage of preparation to the final selection. It gives guidelines and advice on how to get the most out of the interview process and, in so doing, how to get the most out of each candidate. You will then have enough information on each candidate to decide who is the best match for the job on offer and for your organisation. *The Interviewer's Book* will give you answers to common questions that we are both asked regularly, such as:

- How can I connect with the candidate in a meaningful way and get below the surface to discover the real person behind the application?
- How can I remain fair, objective and focussed?
- What kinds of questions should I ask or avoid asking?
- What is the latest thinking about this 'competency-based interviewing' that so many recruiters are using?

- How can I work best with other interviewers to make sure we are all happy with the decision?

Each chapter is structured so that the thinking behind our approach is laid out at the beginning. There are also sections towards the end of each chapter that give summary tips relevant to that chapter's content: details on current best thinking are given in 'what the pros say'; there are details of what 'the best interviewers' do; details of things you should avoid are provided in 'the lazy interviewer' section; and things that you might try or think further about are outlined in the 'coaches' corner'. These lists will be especially helpful as reminders to the reader just before an interview.

We are passionate about the importance of choosing the right person for any available job. A suitably motivated and talented employee or manager will make a valuable contribution to the success of your company or organisation. We have worked with so many people at all levels in organisations who have the opportunity for personal growth and fulfilment by virtue of being suitably matched with a role that allows them to reach their potential and, thereby, enhance the quality of their life hugely. There is great joy and satisfaction in knowing that you had some part to play in making selection decisions that can lead people towards that level of fulfilment.

Mary Hanson and *Brian McIvor*

1

Why You Have to Get
the Interview Right

Provoking Questions

- *Have you ever had the experience of finding that someone you thought was a winner at interview turned out to be a real disappointment, either to you or others, after you hired them?*
- *Have you worked alongside a new recruit and wondered who was foolish enough to think this person was up to the job?*

In this chapter you will learn how to:

- Appreciate the importance of choosing the right candidate
- Put the interview centre stage
- Recognise which type of interviewer you are
- Get yourself in the right frame of mind to take on the responsibility of interviewing

Real-life Experience

John was a real winner when you interviewed him. He spoke highly of the area he had worked in previously; he was an excellent communicator and likeable to the point of being entertaining at the interview; he gave an impressive account of the skills he thought he would bring to the job and professed himself to be willing and ready to make a valuable contribution ...

The reality several months after you hired him was quite different. After the 'honeymoon' period he seemed to be lacking some of the enthusiasm he had shown at interview. He was slow to meet deadlines and seemed to need a lot of clarification and guidance to the point where he frustrated colleagues who had to spend quite a bit of time explaining things to him. Although he was quite sociable at office events, he could also be a hindrance to the team with his constant chatting.

His boss now wants HR to fire him, and everybody's asking, 'Who let him in? Was it you?'

Versions of John's story are replicated all over the corporate world. They point to the challenge that faces all managers throughout their working careers: *how to hire the right person*.

Why Getting It Right Is Important

The investment in hiring, training and orientating a new member of your staff is hugely significant: it takes time and effort on the part of supervisors and colleagues to bring a new recruit up to speed. Even if your new hire performs well enough to stay on your payroll, but is less than excellent in work performance, there is a big accumulated cost: a 20 per cent loss of potential productivity over a working life is a big sum! If the new employee is unable to meet the demands of the job, then time has to be spent on remedial work, coaching, managing performance and, perhaps, eventual dismissal, with all its attendant emotional and legal difficulties. Both the employer and the employee lose out if it gets to that point. It may end up that the new recruit leaves under a cloud, despite perhaps having done their best to match up to the requirements of the job and, having left under those circumstances, they may find it hard to convince another employer of their worth. For the company, it's an admission that they got the hire wrong; it weakens the credibility of the hiring manager and is unsettling for colleagues.

The Role of the Interview in Helping to Choose the Right Person

It is interesting to note that over a long number of years the interview has retained its place amongst employers as the primary method for selecting new staff. Over time it has evolved and developed, and has been influenced by research on its effectiveness. When handled well it is planned, structured and includes a range of probing questions that provide useful and relevant information about the candidate. At the other end of the spectrum it may be a rambling monologue from either the interviewee or the interviewer, or a quick-fire quiz, and can even become embroiled in criticism for being legally discriminatory.

So, when we speak of the 'interview' what do we mean?

We are talking about an exchange between a job applicant and a representative of the hiring company, a structured conversation with a purpose, where both parties have as their agenda a desire to answer the following question:

Is this the right person for the job and the right job for this person?

The Interview Challenge

In the process of selecting a candidate for your company you will come across several types of people, some of whom will be in full sales mode and, like all good salespeople, will try to sell their best features and conceal their faults. The challenge for the interviewer in these circumstances is twofold:

1. How can they get beneath the candidate's 'sales mask' and get a good reading on the realities of them as a potential employee?
2. How can they ensure that the job is right for the candidate and will provide enough scope for personal development to engage the new recruit into the medium term? After all, you don't want to find yourself facing the same challenge of recruitment in a couple of months' time because your new recruit has quit!

You may not always have the luxury of being able to provide richly rewarding work to all new recruits, however, and some of the work on offer may be very repetitive or undemanding. In this case there is no sense in hiring an ambitious, self-driven individual, who will be bored after day 1 in the job. Nevertheless, in some cases you may be able to hire someone who is both ambitious and driven but prepared to undertake basic work for a year or two in the hope that it will lead to a more substantial opportunity. The key point is that the interview should address whether there is a suitable match between the candidate and the job, both in the short and medium term.

Which Type of Interviewer Are You?

Most of us will admit to finding the process of job interviewing challenging, tiring and sometimes haphazard. Some of us will admit to being inadequate as interviewers or at least to having had niggling doubts about our interviewing abilities, yet we all know that we can't escape the inevitable: virtually all team leaders, managers and owner-managers will have to conduct an interview at some point, and many will do it countless times over the course of their working lives. Interviewers come in all shapes and forms; below are some of the types we have come across over the years. Can you spot a striking resemblance to yourself in any of these descriptions?

The Newbie

You are probably reading this book because you have to do your first interview very soon, and the prospect terrifies you! You are not on your own: newer, less-experienced managers often approach interviews with dread. They fret over what questions they should ask and how they can cut through the polished exterior of the groomed and schooled interviewee to get to the heart of what lies beneath.

Yet, determined applicants who are anxious to nail that job will put time, effort and money into preparing for the interview; they will have paid to have their CV polished up, got coaching on how to present at interview and will be prepared to answer the myriad of 'favourite' interview questions. As the interviewer, you will need to excel similarly.

> If the interviewee is that well prepared, you as the interviewer need to be even better prepared! This book will show you the basics and will help you prepare for even the most challenging interviews.

Ms Doubtful

You dread the whole interview process. Over the years you have witnessed first-hand many recruitment failures, and you are unable to believe it is possible to use the interview as a reliable vehicle for hiring new staff. When you interviewed large numbers of staff in the past, you found it hard to differentiate between most of the candidates and could only decide who the absolute worst or best were. You are at a loss to know whether an interview can give you all the insights you need about interviewees so you can make the right choice. Using standardised questions hasn't helped you much. You wonder if interviews serve a useful purpose, and you are tempted to ask why bother interviewing at all. You might as well just pull a number of CVs out of the proverbial hat as your final list!

This book will help you to extend your breadth, range and depth of questions and introduce you to the power of rapport and the skill of reading non-verbal behaviour or 'body language'. You will learn how to assess candidates more comprehensively and accurately. You will also learn how to screen CVs and application forms so that your list of interviewees will be manageable.

Mr Busy

As a key manager you are frequently called upon to interview new staff. Although you can see the benefit of this, it is not a job you welcome. You see it as something that has to be endured because it is just not reasonable to ask anyone else to select a new recruit on your behalf. You are often resentful of the time you have to take out of your normal working week to interview potential staff.

Selecting the right staff is a key management function and makes life far easier for the manager in the long run. The ideal of any manager is to have a cadre of skilled and motivated staff who can produce quality work, while the manager spends the bulk of their time providing resources, feedback and other supports needed to get the job done. So, the manager becomes the conductor of the orchestra rather than a main player! Your best insurance against performance problems in the future is to hire the right staff in the first place, and you will need to invest serious time and effort to be a successful interviewer. This book will help you make the right investment!

The Pro

You have been interviewing for many years and take the job seriously; it is one of your key functions and not one that you would delegate willingly. You prepare properly for interviews by reading applications carefully. You have always been driven by your sense of responsibility to your organisation to select people who will be able to do the job, fit in and grow in your organisation. You are not afraid to probe or guide the interviewee. You enjoy the challenge of finding new talent. Many of your appointees have done well, and you have derived great personal satisfaction from seeing them develop and advance within the organisation, knowing that you were responsible for giving them a start on this path to success through making the initial decision to hire them.

> While you are clearly at the top of your interviewing game, this book may prove to be a useful refresher or provide you with some fresh thinking on how you go about interviewing.

So, then … Which type of interviewer are you?

Do you recognise yourself in any of the above descriptions or are you in a category of your own? Where are you on the road between newbie and pro? The following chapters will provide you with the essential skills and knowledge you need to do the job properly.

Are You Ready to Interview?

Look at the question closely for a minute; what do we mean by being ready?

- Do you have an in-depth understanding of the role to be filled; are you clear on what you need to know to do the job legally; and are you ready to cope with the challenges that interviewees will present, from poor evidence and unclear communication to misrepresentation and downright lying?
- Can you deal with these situations professionally, so that you will give the interviewee a fair hearing, but also properly challenge an interviewee who is prepared to bend the rules to get a job?
- Are you ready to take on the task of identifying a key asset to your company?

If you doubt that you have any of the skills needed to do this key job properly, read on.

What the pros say:

- The interview is still the preferred choice as the main method of choosing the right person to fill a vacancy, despite the fact that it is not an exact science and not 100 per cent reliable.
- Structured, planned interviews are more reliable in selecting effective people than unstructured, unplanned interviews.
- A focus on interviewee competencies within the interview, along with a trawl through the background, experience, interests, disposition, motivation and personal circumstances of the applicant will provide a thorough basis for assessing candidates.

- Past experience is a good predictor of future performance, so interviewers need to delve into the specifics of *what* the candidate has worked at and *how* they approached that work.
- A successful selection decision is more likely if the interview is supplemented with other selection aids, such as aptitude tests, work samples, presentations, etc. that help to provide an even more comprehensive picture of the candidate.
- Getting the right person is key to the health and success of your company or organisation; it is a serious business that requires lots of preparation, time commitment and energy.

The lazy interviewer: ✕

- Sees the interview as a nuisance to be got through as speedily as possible
- Puts their own immediate need to fill a gap ahead of getting the right person in the long run
- Believes all selection decisions should be delegated to the Human Resources department to take the pressure off them

The best interviewers:

- Make sure they understand the full significance of a good or bad hire
- Appreciate that interviewing is not a nuisance that gets in the way of the day job, but rather is an integral part of their role as managers, supervisors and team leaders

- Develop the necessary knowledge and skills of interviewing to optimise their chances of making the soundest hiring decisions
- Invest lots of time in the selection process in the full knowledge that it will pay dividends in the long run

Coaches' Corner – Things for You to Try

- Think about people you may have hired in the past and whether they performed as you expected. If not, how might you have got a more accurate view of the person when you were interviewing them?
- Talk to others who have interviewed and share 'war stories' as a way of motivating you to interview well.
- Search out role models who are known to be good at selecting the right people and talk to them about what they do well as interviewers.
- Get your head in the right place before you get involved in selecting new staff; it's a huge responsibility and the positive and negative consequences are enormous.

2

First Things First – Knowing What You're Looking For and Spreading the Word

Provoking Questions

- *How will you know you have found the right person if you don't know exactly what you're looking for?*
- *How will you get the message out to would-be applicants that you are looking to fill a vacancy?*

In this chapter you will learn how to:

- Decide what you're looking for
- Write a job description and person spec
- Set out the selection criteria you will use
- Draw up a job ad to attract the right candidates
- Use the right channels to get the word out

Real-life Experience

'I deserve a better job than this,' said Ryan, the cashier, as he handed Sophie, the HR Consultant, her lunch in the company canteen; he did not know who he was talking to. Sophie said nothing, but silently agreed. She knew he had a very specialised IT degree but made a mental note to talk to the restaurant manager who had hired Ryan. Were suitable staff that hard to get – in a recession? Had anybody got what they needed out of this poor hiring?

Take a Good Look at What You Need

You have a vacancy: either someone has left and needs to be replaced or work has expanded enough to have created a new role. If you are filling a vacancy, before you go any further take a good look at the job and how it was done previously and see if you need to tweak the requirements based on your experience with the last job holder. Ask yourself the following questions:

- Do you need more or less of certain qualifications, experience or skills this time?
- How much time can you allow for someone to settle into the job and start to deliver results?
- How much coaching and training can you provide to the newcomer?
- Are there circumstances that will point you towards certain personality traits or a particular skill? For instance, if you have a team that is not currently well motivated, you might favour a candidate with really good team-building

skills over and above someone with excellent technical knowledge in order to get the team on track.

- Will the job develop and change much in the months and years ahead, and will the skill requirements change too? If so, you may need to assess candidates' future potential as well as current competence.
- At the same time, don't overreact to the type of person that previously held the position. For example, if the last job holder was overly introverted and difficult to get on with, you shouldn't automatically favour a candidate with an extrovert, sociable nature this time to the detriment of getting someone with high levels of other necessary skills.

It's Good to Talk

Use exit interviews with previous job holders to your advantage. Talk to the previous jobholder before they leave and find out their views on how the job could be made better: could it be made more challenging or less stressful? The person's reason for leaving will prove a useful insight at a time when they can afford to be honest with you. Were they too tightly or loosely managed? Were the goals and targets too undemanding or too stretching? Did the job holder have skills that could have been used but weren't?

Talk to the supervising manager, colleagues and others who have worked with the job holder, such as suppliers or clients, to solicit their views on what they need from the new job holder.

Now sit down and write a job description that tells the full story of what is involved in the job.

What's the Job?

There are several definitions and variations of a 'job description' or 'role profile'. For your purposes as an interviewer you need to examine the job you want done in detail and write down exactly what you want the new person to do, starting with the most important function and working down to the most basic. If you work in a big organisation this may have already been documented. The job description should include detail of the range and scope of the job, and each main task should be identified in a clear and concrete way that spells out exactly what needs to be done by the new employee and *for what purpose*.

Step One: Describe the Job and Draw Up a Role Profile

Listed in the following table is a selection of four of the many tasks that a customer care team leader might have to do on a regular basis:

Customer Care Team Leader Tasks

Task 1	*Seek monthly feedback from customers* via phone calls, surveys and social media, so as to get an accurate and current picture of the level of satisfaction with the service provided.
Task 2	*Analyse and maintain accurate records* of complaints and use them to identify what changes are required by staff in future.

(Continued)

Customer Care Team Leader Tasks: (*Continued*)

Task 3	*Give feedback* to staff on survey results *and agree a plan* of action with them.
Task 4	*Plan and manage weekly team meetings* to ensure that everyone knows what's going on, what needs to be achieved and who needs to do what from one week to the next.

Continue the list to include all the main elements of the role that you want the new hire to do.

Step Two: Describe the Person (The Person Spec)

Now look at the range of skills, knowledge, training, qualifications and behavioural characteristics that are needed to do the job well. The knowledge, training and qualifications needed are normally self-evident, but the other skills may be harder to decide on. Start by looking down through the list of roles or tasks you have outlined, and ask yourself how a competent job holder would perform those tasks well. Group similar skills and competencies under one heading. The following is a simple example of the skills and behaviours needed by our customer care team leader based on the four tasks listed above:

Person Specification for Elements of Customer Care Team Leader Role

Task 1	**Seek Monthly Feedback from Customers**	
	Knowledge	Feedback techniques and latest thinking on customer care
	Skills	Analytical skills for examining options and courses of action
	Behaviour	Customer focussed; handles feedback constructively

Task 2	**Analyse and Maintain Accurate Records**	
	Knowledge	Services/products provided to customers and how they are to be sold
	Skills	Analytical skills for examining information carefully and drawing accurate conclusions
	Behaviour	Attention to detail; organised and systematic approach

Task 3	**Give Feedback to Staff and Agree a Plan**	
	Knowledge	Roles and responsibilities of individuals
	Skills	Leadership and feedback skills
	Behaviour	Communicates clearly

Task 4	Plan and Manage Weekly Team Meetings	
	Knowledge	Motivation techniques and how to use them
	Skills	Presentation and chairing skills
	Behaviour	Gives relevant and timely information; manages time well

This exercise can be extended to include all of the main tasks required by the job function, so you should end up with a comprehensive picture of what you want from the ideal candidate. This will also include the essential knowledge, qualifications and work record that will be needed to do the job. In the case of the customer care team leader, this may include:

- A business degree
- Experience of working in a customer service environment
- Experience of working in a company in the same sector
- Knowledge of feedback and survey tools and techniques so as to get valid and reliable feedback data from customers

> Now that you are clear on what you are looking for, you can set about getting the word out that you are in hiring mode.

In drawing up your specification for the ideal candidate you may want to distinguish between essential and desirable elements of your wish list; for instance, the need to have worked in the same sector might be of value but may not be a deal-breaker, while lack of team-leading skills would be.

What a Good Job Advert Includes

You want to alert potentially good candidates that you are hiring. You need to get that message across clearly in a job advertisement and phrase it in such a way that it attracts those who might be both suitable and interested, yet discourages those who stand no chance of being selected. What you want is a core group of apparently suitable candidates from which you will have a choice of excellent people.

The advertisement should be clear and non-discriminatory (see Chapter 9) and needs to catch the attention of the reader. Give as much detail as you can so people can decide whether the position is worth pursuing or not.

Most job ads include the following:

- The job title
- A general summary of the role
- Some background information about the company, especially anything noteworthy, such as being in a period of rapid expansion or transformation
- A sense of the working culture – paint a picture of the organisation's atmosphere and ethos
- Details of the qualifications, experience and personal qualities being sought
- Information on who to apply to, in what format and by when; don't leave too long a lapse of time or you may lose some good candidates to other job offers, but do give reasonable time for motivated candidates to provide a well-constructed application. Two weeks usually works well.
- Details of any special requirements; these are best pointed out at the advertising stage so the potential

candidate can make a more informed decision about whether to apply, e.g. unsocial hours, requirement to travel, working in a high-pressure environment, etc.

The amount of information you give will, to some extent, depend on where you decide to advertise and what your budget is. You might choose to put less information in the ad itself but direct people to your website for further details. This can be a huge help to potential candidates who can assess the company in some detail before deciding to apply.

Where To Go Fishing

Advertising for an employee in the right way can save you a lot of time and trouble. The challenge is to get your message across to the right people, but not too many or too few. You may have several choices open to you, as follows:

Word of mouth: there is no cost involved, but be wary: you may end up with 'cliques' or groups of staff whose personal loyalties to each other outweigh their loyalty to the company. Also, you may end up with too many similar types of people (e.g. from the same area or from the same previous company) and miss out on getting people from a diverse range of backgrounds.

Finder system: some companies operate a finder's fee, whereby they reward staff for introducing a potentially suitable candidate. This can work well if it is clear that staff should only recommend people whom they are confident can perform. Many companies delay paying some or all of the finder's fee till the recommended person has successfully passed their period of probation.

Advertising locally: this will keep the numbers of applicants down, as local people will know the company and may already have a view on whether they would like to work there. It will be attractive to those who do not want to spend too much time commuting to work, and this may also be advantageous to the company.

Advertising in a specialist journal: this allows you to target a particular group. It is particularly useful when you are looking for someone with a professional qualification, such as engineers, architects, psychologists, pharmacists, etc.

Using your own database: you may wish to trawl through a retained list of applicants who contacted you within the past few months, or look back on results of other recent recruitment campaigns to see if there is anyone suitable whom you could contact to find out if they are still interested in working for you.

Conventional advertising, such as newspapers, radio or television: cost may be the greatest consideration in using any of these vehicles for your advertisement. Local media are cheaper than national media, however, and may be more targeted. Sometimes the cost of a big ad in a national newspaper may be worth it if you want to use it for PR purposes also, i.e. to advertise your product or to tell the nation that you are in a period of growth. If you are using a national newspaper to advertise your job, issues of size, design, the position of the ad on the page and the day of the week that it will appear will all need to be considered.

Job fairs: most major urban centres are host to regular job fairs, which allow employers to exhibit their wares, provide personalised information about their company and perhaps make presentations to would-be job applicants. The one-to-one contact with jobseekers can be especially useful, particularly if your company's representative is well chosen for the role.

Recruitment agencies: specialised recruitment agencies can be used to help design a job ad or to get a ready-made shortlist of potential candidates. The quality of the service you receive will depend on you putting time into briefing the agency carefully on what you want and making it clear that you want them to screen candidates rigorously to come up with a realistic shortlist. As with any contracting of services, you should stay in the driving seat and also drive a hard bargain!

Using Available Technologies

Employers have the opportunity to use current technologies to full advantage when it comes to hiring new employees.

Company Website

To start with you can advertise online through your company's website. The website can be developed to include links to sources of information that might be of use to candidates, and could include lots of helpful information about:

- The company and its products or services
- Current issues or developments, or recent achievements
- Details of codes of practice, policy statements and other HR information
- Video clips to give a visual story, which could include clips of recent new hires detailing how they are settling into their jobs

You will need to consider how you will attract or prompt people to browse your website, unless you are in a large, well-known company that has a popular website. You will also want to plan how you can handle queries: do you want to give a contact number and name or would it be better to direct inquiries to an email address specially set up for this recruitment drive?

Job Search Websites

There are countless job search websites and boards available to jobseekers, and your vacancy can be posted on any of these. Some websites use sophisticated search engines to pull listings from thousands of other websites, including jobs boards, company career sites, newspapers, government sites, etc. Choose a site that is suitable for your line of business. You should provide enough information to give possible applicants a good sense of what the job involves and what the company is like to work for, and refer them to your own website if you have one that is of use to potential applicants. Many job search websites also have refined search facilities that will home in on any special features that a jobseeker is particularly looking for, so careful wording of your ad to mention special features of the role will steer some of the most appropriate candidates to your company. Be prepared for recruitment agencies to contact you to make a pitch for your business when they see you advertising on these sites.

Social Media

Many job vacancies are first heard of through social media. On almost all the large job search websites a jobseeker can link in with their Twitter or Facebook accounts to get regular updates on suitable vacancies. This means that you can get a very instant result when you advertise. Word can get around even before you want it to!

Professional networking sites such as LinkedIn can act as a jobs board where employers post vacancies. As with job search websites, jobseekers can usually use key words to target a search for suitable jobs on these sites.

Some employers like to use social networking sites such as Twitter as a vehicle for reaching out to people. If you plan to use social networking as part of your recruitment campaign, you may wish to consult a professional marketing company that can help ensure you are targeting the right people. Social networking is most beneficial where your company's account is being used as a marketing/PR tool with lots of activity and regular updates and interaction with followers. It may not be the panacea, but it is an affordable way of reaching out to a large audience.

A downside of social media is that you may get a lot of unwanted applications. To reduce the risk of this, ask the applicant to give an account of exactly why they want the job and to outline and match their experience and skills to the main elements of your job description.

What the pros say: ✓

- Time spent at the very early stage of recruitment in planning what you're looking for and how you're going to look for it is time well spent.
- Developing a job spec is not an old-fashioned, academic exercise; it gives you a rigorous means of working through what you want from the position and from the new job holder.
- Use advances in technology to your advantage.

The lazy interviewer: ✗

- Uses the same advertisement as the last time
- Draws on an old job description for details of the job
- Uses the same advertising provider as before without looking at what the level of response was from that source
- Emails a recruitment company with a request for CVs without giving the consultant any in-depth briefing
- Contacts candidates from a previous recruitment short-list, despite the fact that the essentials of the job have changed in the meantime

The best interviewers: ✓

- Spend time looking at what exactly the job involves before starting to recruit
- Check that they haven't made the selection criteria either too demanding or too loose
- Design a job advertisement carefully to attract just the right candidates
- Use relevant media strategically to get the optimum coverage for their job ad
- Seek to spread the recruitment net just wide enough to get neither too few nor too many interested applicants

Coaches' Corner – Things for You to Try

- Reflect on previous hires and see if there is anything you learned from those experiences that will affect how you deal with this recruitment campaign.
- Try to make your vacancy notice a bit different or novel.
- Look at job ads from other companies to see what works well.
- Look at the websites of companies that are advertising for staff and see what information they put on their site for potential applicants.
- Keep up to speed with what's happening in the world of recruitment by trawling through job search websites to see what's hot (or not!) in the online marketplace.
- Familiarise yourself with qualifications and educational institutions in the specialist field you are recruiting for.
- Anticipate how jobs will expand over time: what new skills and knowledge will the holder need in the future?

3

From Mountain to Molehill – Shortlisting

Provoking Question

- *How can you sort that huge bundle of applications into a small number for interview?*

In this chapter you will learn how to:

- Read applications and CVs more insightfully
- Get a shortlist together in an objective way

Real-life Experience

It was nine o'clock at night, and Dara had hundreds of CVs to plough through and a shortlist of no more than ten names to put forward for interview; the pressure was on to contact people no later than tomorrow. There were a couple of obvious stars at the top end and some timewasters at the other extreme, but what about all those other CVs? He began to sort them into three piles headed 'yes', 'no' and 'maybe', but how on earth was he going to decide who should make the cut from that middle pile? It looked like he would be up all night if he wanted to get this right!

Reading Applications and CVs More Insightfully

What the Application or CV Tells You on the Surface

A candidate's written application can give you a preliminary picture that may include the following:

- Some biographical detail
- Education level, results and type of qualification
- Level, depth and range of work experience
- Specific job skills
- Writing skills
- Patterns of achievement and rate of career progress
- Special interests and preferences

Application Form or CV?

If you use your own application form you can design it to get more consistent information in the same format from all applicants. Good application forms will ask some searching questions about the candidate's motivation and fit with the position.

CVs provide candidates with more flexibility about what information they provide (or don't provide) and how they present it. You can always ask for CVs to include specific information so that you are sure to get what you need to make an informed decision about whom to shortlist. A CV can also be used to do a preliminary check on a candidate's ability to present information logically and clearly but, of course, you have to bear in mind that it may have been touched up by a professional. Look for evidence of motivation to get this particular job in how the CV is constructed: has the candidate taken the time to gear it towards your vacancy, or are they using a one-size-fits-all approach to job hunting?

Reading Between the Lines

It's hard to assess 'soft data' about someone's personality, behaviour or special attributes, but you can use the CV or application form to examine education and work experience in some detail before making preliminary decisions about who you will take a further look at.

Education

- Look at the results in detail – a high honours graduate is likely to be more technically competent and hard-working than someone with a more average result.
- Look at the university or college attended – some have higher standards and demand more of their students, and some specialise in certain disciplines.
- Be suspicious of 'diplomas' from second- and third-rate colleges – check who the awarding body is.
- Did the candidate succeed in getting through the course in the minimum number of semesters?

Experience

- Look at the length and depth of experience and how much responsibility the candidate had.
- Are there indications of results achieved; has the candidate worked at different levels?
- Is all experience in the one sector?
- How varied has the experience been? What types of companies has the candidate worked for in terms of size, type of product or service, market standing, ethos, etc.?
- Look for a sense of progress, advancement and achievement when you look at the experience.

Specific Job Skills and Special Aptitudes

Probe the application for indications of particular skills, such as project management, team leading, customer sales, managing change, or implementing new technologies or work processes.

Lifestyle

Information may be given on interests and leisure activities, and this information can give you some insights as to the following:

- Sociability – introvert or extrovert?
- Balanced lifestyle
- Physical fitness
- Interest in intellectual, artistic, sporting, political or community activities

While someone's leisure activities are their own concern, you can get some sense of the type of person you are dealing with by knowing what their likes and preferences are. It is not important whether someone prefers soccer to rugby, but it is reassuring to know that a candidate has a healthy, balanced lifestyle that allows them to relax outside of work hours and enhances their physical health and mental wellbeing. You can also look to see if someone has skills that are not used in work but are demonstrated through leisure activities. Take care though that you don't jump to any biased conclusions; for instance, just because a candidate plays a team sport doesn't mean de facto that they are a good team member; they may cause untold frustration to other team members by not showing enough commitment, not being reliable, not sharing their expertise, etc.

Getting the Shortlist Together

Sometimes it will be easy to separate your pile of applications into obvious groups of 'yes' and 'no' candidates. However, a single yardstick may not always be discriminating enough to give you that obvious division. You may still find you have too many people in the 'yes' bundle to call for interview. Now the dilemma is how much further you want to delve into the applications to get to the gold.

The basic standard of shortlisting goes something like this:

Shortlisting or Shortcutting?

John has received almost four hundred CVs for a vacancy on his sales team. He scans the first 50 or so and sees a few that look really good at first sight – well put together, with good experience and qualifications – and he has a sense that they give off a general air of being top-class candidates. He stops there, as he reckons that's enough of a field from which to pick a winner and, in any event, he doesn't want to spend more than a day at interviewing.

John may well get a suitable candidate, but he has no way of knowing whether there are other star candidates that he missed. From a pragmatic point of view, that may be fine, but many companies would want to know that a more objective, rigorous approach to shortlisting was applied, and that if any applicant queried why they weren't selected they would be able to provide a reasonable answer.

A further refinement to John's approach would involve going through all the applications and sorting them into three categories: 'yes', 'no' and 'maybe'. At least this approach ensures all CVs are read, but you may still end up with too many or too few in the 'yes' category, and what criteria have you used as the basis for this categorising?

If you want to be rigorous in the way you shortlist, you need to go further than either of the above approaches. You will have to go back to the job description and person spec and draw up a basic set of selection criteria to use for shortlisting. You will also need to construct a marking scheme.

Simple Shortlisting Scheme

The easiest, most objective criteria for deciding which candidates you will take a further look at will centre on aspects of either education or work experience. Perhaps you have one or two very exacting factors you are not prepared to compromise on, and that may automatically generate an adequate shortlist, as the following examples demonstrate:

Example 1

I am the head of the ladies clothing department in a retail store. I want to hire a good sales assistant. I will give preference to any of the applicants who have worked for a department store, who have experience of dealing with certain fashion labels and who have a third-level qualification in retail fashion or fashion buying.

Example 2

I am the head of a radio station that is looking for a good DJ. I know I will get a flood of CVs from about five thousand wannabe DJs, but I have decided that I will consider only those who already have radio experience and can prove it by quoting programme and station names.

Applying relevant selection criteria, as in the above examples, will inevitably reduce the number of viable applications.

Using a More Detailed Rating Scheme for Shortlisting

In many cases the use of one or two basic criteria will not be enough to choose between candidates. The table overleaf shows how you might delve deeper into each CV; it is a template designed for shortlisting candidates for a software

Shortlisting Criteria for Software Engineer

Criteria	Sub-criteria	Total Marks		Max
Education*	Primary degree in physics, maths, computer science, general or software engineering, or similar	1st Class Honours 2:1 Honours 2:2 Honours Pass	60 40 30 20	60
	Masters degree in any of the above subject areas	1st Class Honours 2:1 Honours 2:2 Honours	60 40 30	60
	Other masters (e.g. business)	Honours or Pass	20	
Training*	Certified technical training courses	Maximum	40	40
Experience	Number of years experience as software engineer/developer	Per year of experience (max 3)	20	90
	Experience of working on a particular system or application	Maximum	30	
*Allocate fewer marks for a less valued college, or if the candidate took more than the minimum number of years to complete the course; tweak this section on education depending on the calibre of education you expect.		Total		250

engineering vacancy suitable for a graduate engineer with a few years' work experience where you are dealing with a large pool of applicants.

You could collapse the marks within each of the sections in the table opposite and have three broad ratings only, as follows:

Broad Shortlisting Criteria for Software Engineer

Criteria	Mark
Education	120
Training	40
Experience	90
Total	250

CVs To Be Wary Of

When shortlisting, you should be cautious of CVs that:

- Look too generic, with no evidence of being matched to the job specification
- Have content that has obviously been cut and pasted from other sources
- Are too long-winded
- Are hard to follow and extract clear information from

Our CV Pet Hates

- CVs that include sweeping statements, or any of these phrases: 'excellent communications skills', 'good team member', 'diligent' or 'hard-working'

- CVs that have multiple narrative statements starting with 'I'
- CVs that are bound with heavy-duty plastic covers
- Cheesy photographs
- Multiple typos
- The words CURRICULUM VITAE in large type – as if that was the applicant's name!
- Multiple implausible referees or name dropping
- CVs with cover letters that include phrases like:
  - You will not regret hiring me.
  - There is no need to look at any other application.
  - Please give me a job! I really need this job badly.
  - If you don't give me this job, I may do something drastic!

What the pros say:

- Put time and effort into shortlisting in the knowledge that it is time well spent.
- Apply a rigorous approach to dealing with all applications.
- Two heads are better than one!
- Employers often tend to hire clones – people who are like them – on the basis that they will fit in better with the company and, in so doing, they miss the opportunity to hire staff who have different approaches and ways of thinking.

The lazy interviewer: ✗

- Randomly selects a small number of applications for shortlisting and throws the rest aside without looking at them
- Uses only one criterion for shortlisting; for example, only shortlisting those candidates who have more than x number of years' experience in a very similar job
- Scans the applications and decides which ones to shortlist on the basis of 'gut feeling'
- Picks out only those applications with less than two pages of writing

The best interviewers: ✓

- Decide what's important to the company and to their department or area at the time of recruitment and reflect this in their approach to shortlisting
- Allow themselves plenty of time to go through applications and apply a simple and well-thought-out rating of candidates to get a shortlist, which will be time well spent in the end
- Make a judgement as to what weight to give to work experience, education and special skills, depending on the level they want to hire at
- Review each application carefully and get a sense of the person by reading between the lines
- Don't make up their minds too hastily about excluding any candidate
- Minimise their personal biases in assessing the facts

Coaches' Corner – Things for You to Try

- Look through application forms with a fresh eye and see if you can read between the lines to uncover more of the personal story of each candidate before you ever see them.
- Watch out for the tendency to look for *clones* – applicants who have the same background, education or previous employers as current employees – on the assumption that they are more likely to 'fit in'.
- Give preference to CVs that are logical and professional in layout and content, written in clear language and tailored to the job. Candidates who take the trouble to make their CV more readable might be worth a second look.

4

Game Plan

Provoking Questions

- *Is it a good idea to make a decision on who to hire on the basis of one interview alone?*
- *You hear so many stories about interviews that were handled disastrously by the interviewers: do you know how to plan and structure an interview so you don't mess up?*

In this chapter you will learn how to:

- Decide what type of interview suits your needs
- Best use your resources
- Select the best type of interview
- Decide what other selection tools you should use to supplement the interview
- Plan the sequence and structure of the interview
- Work well with other selectors
- Interview internal candidates or someone you know well

Real-life Experience

Roger had to find himself a new regional sales manager, and urgently! He shortlisted down to five candidates and, along with another sales manager, he interviewed each candidate for 45 minutes, during which time they were given an opportunity to 'sell themselves', as he put it. One of the candidates was an insider – a sales executive who worked for the other interviewer. Roger discounted him despite his colleague's insistence that he had what it takes and was a strong contender. Instead, he was most impressed by the first candidate, who gave a great account of his achievements and worked for the company's main competitor. Could Roger be sure this was the right person for the job based on a short encounter with someone for whom a sales pitch was second nature? His colleague was not impressed with Roger's slipshod approach or his refusal to listen to his views. He would have to try to convince Roger to do it differently next time!

What Type of Interview Best Suits Your Needs?

You have a shortlist of candidates and want to select the best one. The task will have to be tailored to what resources you have and the scale of the recruitment campaign. If you are planning to hire a number of people at once, you may want to use some techniques other than the interview to help you differentiate between them. Even if you limit yourself to using the interview as your only selection vehicle, there are several types of interview which you may choose from.

> The most important thing to remember is: *avoid making a decision to hire based on one interview alone!*

Types of Interview

When it comes to interviewing the shortlisted candidates, there are several options open to you as to how you use your time and that of others involved in the selection process. The list below sets out the options that are available to you.

Option 1: Initial Screening Interview

This is a short, first-stage interview to add to candidates' CV details.

Option 2: Chat and Interview

This is a combination of meeting for an informal chat and a more formal interview. The informal chat can either be used for the same purpose as the screening interview mentioned in Option 1 above, but this is also sometimes held over for the last couple of candidates in the ring. By this stage all the boxes will have been ticked, and the informal chat may be used to get a sense of the totality of the person, perhaps to check their fit with the organisation, or may be used to involve the CEO if they have not been directly involved earlier in the process.

Option 3: Standard Interview

Following on from the screening interview, this is a longer, more thorough interview to assess competence and suitability, usually with more than one interviewer.

Option 4: Sequential and Specialist Interviews

Sequential interviews involve a rolling series of interviews run by different key people who all need to be part of the final decision. Interviews can be either one-to-one or two-to-one. A consensus is then arrived at. A refinement of this involves splitting the interview up into specialist interviews, as follows:

1. The first interview might focus on biographical details and work history.
2. The second interview may be given by a technical expert to assess technical knowledge.
3. The third interview should focus on personal attributes and competencies.

Good communication and briefing of all players is essential so that interviews don't become repetitive for interviewees – each interview should add something extra to the process. Have a plan for how you will merge the information from different interviewers, and be sure you are all on the same page regarding your selection criteria. Many companies overdo the use of sequential interviews and run the risk of frustrating good candidates by asking them to sit through several overly-repetitious interviews with different managers.

Option 5: Board Interview

This is a formal board or panel interview where, typically, three or more people sit together to interview all candidates. When the number of candidates is large, there may be several boards running simultaneously. Each board will have an allocated chairperson and perhaps also a secretary or note-taker; they may also have an external expert to add objectivity. This approach is typically used for large public service competitions. The increased formality attached to this type of interview may get in the way of real engagement and rapport (see Chapter 5 on 'Getting the Chemistry Right' and the impact that formality has on the quality of the information you get from candidates).

Summary

There are several other permutations and combinations of interviews too – the choice is yours. In choosing what is best for you and your organisation, however, bear the following in mind:

- Don't ask candidates to go through too many hoops – you have to balance your wish to be thorough with the candidate's willingness to give you endless time without knowing whether it is going to be worth the effort.
- Whatever your choice, it is going to be a time-consuming process, and there really aren't any shortcuts out there, but just keep remembering that getting the right person is always worth the effort.

- Have a plan for how you will merge the information from different interviewers and be sure you are all on the same page as to what you are looking for.
- A bad hire is an expensive mistake – you can do the sums yourself on the gross salary cost, lower productivity, training and remedial cost of redoing work, rechecking work, time spent on close supervision, resentment of colleagues, etc. It is worth investing time upfront in the process to avoid probation or performance evaluation problems later.

How to Best Use Your Resources for Interviewing

You may have no other resources to call on if you are in a small company. If so, it might be advisable to get the help of a recruitment specialist or, if that is too costly, ask someone whom you know to be a good solid interviewer to assist you.

If there are large numbers of candidates to be interviewed, you may have to set up teams of interviewers.

If many different people need to be involved in the selection decision, they need to plan how they will all have an input. Frequently, the line manager has the ultimate say, but input may be required from others, depending on company policy. Other interested parties and resources would typically include the HR department, the relevant team leader or a potential work colleague with whom the new hire will have to collaborate, and perhaps a customer, client or external expert who can bring some objectivity or technical expertise to the selection process.

Is it best to have three or four people see a candidate separately or for them to interview the candidate together?

Sometimes the best use of available and willing selectors is to stage two interviews with one common link person being involved in both. That way, you can carry out two interviews using three people.

Other Selection Aids

In order to increase the reliability of your selection process, it is worth considering using some different selection aids and not to rely fully on the interview for making your hiring decisions. Of course, there will be considerations of time and cost to take into account, but the use of the aids described below increases your chances of making the right decisions.

Phone Interviews

Structured phone interviews can be used to get more infor-mation from candidates before setting up face-to-face interviews. They can be used selectively and can help to establish particular facts, to seek clarification or to test for an acceptable level of social and communication skills. If you can phone over the Internet and get an opportunity to have visual contact, then all the better. Either way, you will have to make sure you use a broad range of rapport-building techniques to get the conversation off on the right footing. Many companies use phone interviewing to establish candi-dates' levels and types of experience, skills and proficiency with particular software, and to make preliminary enquiries about salary expectations. Phone interviewing can also help ensure that you do not call someone needlessly to interview and waste their time and yours.

Presentations

Asking candidates to make a presentation based on a well-selected topic can be useful for checking their communication skills, persuasiveness and public credibility. You can choose to give the topic in advance or give, say, an hour to the candidate to prepare on the day. Let them know in advance what to expect.

The presentation can also be used to test a candidate's depth of knowledge about a technical subject, to show how they will tackle the main challenges of the job, or to see how they would make a sales pitch for the company's product. Include a robust question and answer session to allow the candidate to field questions and enable you to get a better sense of how they interact, handle pressure and think on the spot.

Regular topics for presentation include the following:

- Do a critical evaluation of the company's strategic plan.
- This company is in recovery mode; explain and justify the changes you foresee that you and the management team would have to implement.
- If you were offered the job, what would your first considerations be? What challenges will you face, and what would your work plan for the first three months look like?

Decide in advance if you want candidates to use Power-Point or not; it might be worth considering not using it to avoid the danger that the presentation will degenerate into a sequence of slides that the candidate will read from. If you ask them to use it, make sure it works!

Personality Questionnaires

These usually measure personal traits that may be essential to successful performance, e.g. level of introversion/extraversion, team qualities, the ability to handle stress, etc. The best personality questionnaires are designed to be reliable and valid, but special training and licensing is required to administer and interpret most of them. Some of the popular tests are not strictly psychological tests, but they give a profile based on a candidate's expressed behaviour preference, e.g. in leadership or conflict situations. However, while some of these tests are very insightful and useful, others are not based on any meaningful research or validation at all, and are best avoided; they are more appropriate to a magazine or online quiz rather than as a serious interview aid. In general, you should use the results of personality questionnaires as part of the overall selection process, to inform what you might ask at interview, rather than as a means of shortlisting.

Aptitude and Ability Tests

These are designed to measure verbal skills, numerical reasoning or mechanical ability. They have the advantage of being objective and well trialled, and they make it easy to compare candidates. There are lots of tests available for very specific business and industrial conditions.

Work Samples and In-tray Exercises

You can ask candidates to bring along some samples of work they have done in the past. For example, if you are hiring a graphic artist or web designer, you would want to see some of their designs. Ask them to be prepared to answer questions on how they went about this work so you can be sure the work is their own. You can also give candidates a piece of relevant work to complete as part of your selection process. You could simulate a task that they may be likely to have to do on the job and see how they tackle it. For instance, if you were planning to hire a PR executive you would like to know that they could write a good press brief, so ask them to prepare one based on some background material that you give them to read on the day.

In-tray exercises can also provide a valuable opportunity to test a candidate's ability to assimilate information quickly and make decisions. Examples of what you could ask them to work on include:

- Assessing contract bids and choosing the best bid
- Deciding on a course of action based on a number of emails
- Preparing a concise brief for a management or board presentation based on documentation provided

Be sure to alert candidates in advance so they know what to expect, but it is best to leave the detail of the task until the day. You'd be amazed at the difference in standard from one person to the next!

Group Exercise

This is where a group of candidates is asked to either do a task together or carry on a discussion on a topic chosen by the recruiter. For instance, the group may be presented with a problem that needs to be solved, or they may be asked to discuss a topic that is likely to generate debate and diverging views. The behaviour of individuals in the group is observed, and their ability to persuade, influence and handle disagreement, as well as their level of self-confidence, can be noted.

Site Visit

A visit around the premises or site can help both parties: the candidate gets a chance to meet future colleagues, validate their impression of the company and make a more informed decision about whether this is the company for them, and the employer gets a chance to check out how the candidate interacts with others, how they listen, how they deal with new faces and whether they ask sensible questions. The recruiter can also use the visit to seek the views of colleagues as to whether they would welcome working with the visitor.

Going All The Way: Assessment Centres

'Assessment centre' is the name given to a collection of activities and exercises, including any or all of the selection aids discussed above, sometimes together with interviews, that are undertaken by candidates, normally over a period of a full day or more. The fact that the candidates are observed through various exercises and in a number of situations gives the recruiters a far better chance of getting a more comprehensive picture, and the candidates tend to relax more over such a lengthy period and be more like their real selves. Because they are so resource intensive, assessment centres tend to be used more for key positions or for senior or middle management positions. Some of the activities are less resource intensive than others, but most assessment centres are time-consuming and may finish with a meal or social function. Companies will sometimes hire experts in recruitment to assist with this process.

What Selection Aids Will Work for You?

There is an array of tools that you can use to supplement the interview, and you are limited only by the old reliables of cost and time considerations. You should never hire on the basis of seeing someone at one interview only, however, and it is advisable to use at least one or two other selection aids alongside the interview to increase your chances of making the right decision. You also need to consider how much time you expect the applicants to invest in the selection process: if it is too demanding of their time they may withdraw before the final hurdle, particularly if they are working in a busy environment where they may find it difficult to take a lot of time off. Remember, you may not be the only company they are applying to at the same time.

Giving Structure to the Interview

The secret to good interviewing lies in developing a structured approach to the interview. Planning beforehand to put a structure on the interview gives you certainty that you have covered all the relevant areas and helps you to manage your use of interview time. It helps to get yourself on track and keep you there and is useful in getting you motivated and focussed on the task and the outcomes you want. It also helps the interviewee to participate more fully, as the structure allows them to give a comprehensive account of themselves.

Before You Interview

Decide what you're looking for: you won't be able to interview well unless you know what you're looking for, so some thinking time before the interview is critical. You want to go into the interview with a good idea of the behaviours and competencies you need the ideal candidate to have in order to perform the job well.

Plan your approach: how many interviews should you do, what type of interviews will you conduct, and who will be involved? Schedule time as you would for a project, but always be generous in the time you allocate. Allow enough time for:

- Discussion with other interviewers
- Familiarising yourself with applications
- The interview itself – it will be difficult to make much headway in less than 45 minutes, even for jobs at junior level, and, of course, many applicants for more senior or complex jobs will need far more time to give an account of their experience and fit with the job on offer.
- The after-interview assessment of candidates (which should be done after each interview and not piled up till the end of the day). Interviewers *always* underestimate how long this can take. Allow a gap of at least 20 minutes between each interview.

Brief other interviewers: divide the work between you so that all bases are covered and everyone is clear on who has to do what. Play to your colleagues' strengths in dividing the work, and agree how you are going to work together.

Prepare the scene: see Chapter 5 for guidelines on setting up a good physical environment for the interview.

Do your homework: spend whatever time it takes to read carefully through each candidate's application. Become familiar with the contents to the point where you won't have to look down at it too often during the interview itself. Note any areas of the application that you want to pursue in detail or want another interviewer to pursue.

Phases of the Interview

Phase 1: Warm Up

This part of the interview sets the tone. You should greet the candidate and make quick introductions. Try to make a special effort to connect – it's not just a nice thing to do but an essential part of getting the interview on track early and giving the candidate an opportunity to relax into a natural version of themselves. Use your best rapport-building skills, such as a friendly tone of voice, a smile, direct eye contact, use of first names, etc. These skills will be covered in more detail in Chapter 5.

This early part of the interview may also be used to explain what the job is all about, what the candidate can expect, what the interview plan is, and who will be talking about what. However, don't labour the formalities too much, as some candidates will be anxious to press on with the interview proper, especially if they have had other interview experiences and already have a good idea of how the interview will be handled. Also, if they have received good information about the job and the company from you beforehand, you won't need to go into any detail about the job on offer until a later point when the candidate may wish to get certain clarifications.

Phase 2: Exploring the CV

Begin with a biographical approach, giving the candidate the chance to settle down by asking them to give you a quick summary of their background and CV details.

Ask them to *briefly* highlight the areas of their experience and expertise that are most relevant; if they have a long CV with various jobs this is a good way of homing in on the relevant aspects and leaving the dross aside.

This part of the interview will give you some leads to follow up on, so you can put the questions you want to ask into context. For instance, if the candidate highlights a particular project as one of their achievements, you might come back to it later as a vehicle for asking about organisation skills, behaviour in teams, technical competence, etc.

Phase 3: Exploring Competencies

Match the candidate's experience, qualifications and knowledge to the headings on the job spec. How easy is it to match the job description and the CV? This phase is the heart of the interview, where you seek the interviewee's help in trawling through their experiences to get to the reality of exactly what they have done and how they have done it. Chapters 6–8 give more extensive detail on how to ask the right questions to get a true sense of what the candidate's level of skill, knowledge and personal attributes are.

Phase 4: Selling Your Organisation

The right candidate may have other jobs they are interested in, so be alert to the need to sell the job. If they are someone special, they may be checking you out! In selling your organisation, talk about opportunities for promotion, advancement and development on the job – work environments and how people are managed are critical factors in retaining staff. Stress also the positive nature of the job, the work, brand, profile, customer base, company values and prestige. However, avoid the temptation to oversell the position and risk a mismatch. If there are negatives, such as unsocial hours, a lot of travelling or high pressure deadlines, spell these out clearly and seek the candidate's views on them.

Phase 5: Salary Negotiation and Other Matters

Issues of salary and other aspects of terms and conditions are preferably left till late in the selection process. In many companies, all mention of salary and other terms of employment are handled solely by HR staff. If a salary range has already been quoted in the job ad or accompanying material, there is no need to pursue it any further with the candidate until you are ready to offer a job. If the candidate is not aware of the details of the package on offer, you may need to give an indicative figure so they know whether they are in the ballpark or not. If the salary and benefits you have to offer are standard and unlikely to have room for change, you should be familiar with the details. Don't forget bonuses, fringe benefits, etc. You should also be familiar with industry norms – your candidate will! Take time to explain the package fully to ensure both you and the candidate are comparing like with like.

If there is flexibility on the details of the package depending on the calibre of the candidate, it will not be appropriate to get into negotiations on salary or conditions before you are in a position to make a job offer. If that is the case, just get an indicative figure of what the candidates are expecting and what their current package is. On your side, be careful not to overstep the mark by mentioning figures or perks that cannot be delivered on.

Phase 6: The Conclusion

The temptation is to wrap up the interview prematurely. To add value, at the end of the interview the interviewer can:

- Follow up on areas they may have under-explored earlier
- Sell the job succinctly and subtly
- Ask the candidate if they want to add anything
- Check out how attractive the candidate finds the job and whether they can articulate a vision of how they will contribute to the company's future

Equally, at the end of an interview, the candidate can:

- Make a pitch for the job
- Add any extra information that the interviewers might have missed
- Revisit something they may have been stuck on at an earlier stage in the interview
- Seek further clarification about aspects of the job

Interviewing with Others

As it's not advisable to go solo when it comes to making a hiring decision, you will often be one of a partnership or team of interviewers. Apart from the challenge of finding the right person, you have the added complication of working out how best to play to the strengths of your interviewing partner or team. As a team, you will experience the challenges that all teams face – how to work well together and how best to resolve any differences. You may know your fellow interviewers well and already know how to play to each others' strengths, but in bigger companies this may not be the case. Indeed, in some situations you may be interviewing with a complete outsider, or you may be that outsider who has been asked to help with the interviews.

Ground Rules for Interviewing with Others

- Meet well in advance of interviews to agree what you want from the ideal candidate and, preferably, be collectively involved in shortlisting.

- Be clear on roles – who is responsible for what, who is going to ask what, and how will the grey areas of overlap be handled within the team of interviewers?
- Play to the expertise of each interviewer.
- Ideally, have someone take a lead role in managing the process.
- Whether you designate a leader or not, there are several aspects of the process that someone needs to take responsibility for; these include:
  - Managing the introduction of the interview
  - Managing the interview time
  - Ensuring that the interviewers have all the paperwork they need and that good notes are taken and kept for use afterwards
  - Intervening if the interview goes off-track, doesn't run to time or isn't handled in a fair manner. You will need to agree how this will be done, what 'signal' will be given, and at what point it is acceptable to interrupt proceedings.
  - Ensuring that helpful feedback is given to each interviewer between interviews. If a colleague has been asking useless questions, has been off-putting in attitude to the interviewee or has been inadequate in any other way as an interviewer, they should be given constructive feedback on this.
- Any interpersonal problems between interviewers should be dealt with sensitively but assertively. If not, these difficulties will spill over and get in the way of the real business of the interview. If you are too sensitive about a colleague in such a situation and avoid dealing

with the problem, be in no doubt that it may lead to a poor hiring decision.

Interviewing Your Colleagues – Internal Promotions

Some interviewers and interviewees find interviews more difficult if they know each other well: maybe they have worked together for years, or perhaps they know each other personally. As the interviewer, you may worry about the implications for your future work relationship with this colleague if they do not get the job you interview them for. You know that the interview may be carefully scrutinised by staff and accusations of favouritism and political strokes can fly around all too readily.

Interviewees, for their part, can also find this type of interview uncomfortable; many of them say they would prefer to be interviewed by total strangers. The failure to be chosen for promotion can be a very public humiliation, apart from it being a deep personal disappointment and a perceived negative message about their worth to the company or organisation.

The best way to avoid any negative fallout from internal and promotional interviews is to be on top of your brief, as follows:

- Have a clear road map for what competencies you are looking for and ensure all interviewees know too.
- Make it clear to candidates what part previous experience, performance reviews or references from colleagues will play in your decision-making.

- Have a consistent approach to all the interviews, so each candidate feels they are given the same attention and treatment.
- If you ask the exact same questions, word will filter out, and those interviewed later will be at an advantage; just be sure you cover the same broad areas and that you are consistent in the standard of reply you expect from all interviewees.
- Let interviewees know in advance that the interview process will be a serious in-depth affair and that they cannot take anything for granted. The interview will give them a chance to give a comprehensive account of their track record and their insights as to what they will do in this new job.
- Make sure people in the organisation know the criteria that are used both in pre-selection and at the interview.
- Ensure that candidates are familiar with the company's procedures and policies on promotion.

Some organisations, as a matter of practice, ask the interviewer who is interviewing a colleague to step back from the interview and allow other interviewer(s) to take the lead. However, our preference is for all interviewers to take a full part in the interview. In some situations you may find that you have first-hand experience of the candidate's strengths but that they are not showing them off in the interview. Direct and phrase your questions in a way that allows the interviewee to give an account of what you know they have handled well. By asking questions about situations you know they handled well, you can prompt them to give a good account of themselves. You should do likewise if you have first-hand experience of a candidate who is lacking some of the skills you are looking for: ask questions that will challenge them and will expose what you know to be skill gaps. There is no point in waiting till the interview is over and then trying to convince the other interviewers of a candidate's failings.

If you are interviewing both internal and external candidates you need to allow for the fact that the external candidates will not have as much insight into how your organisation works or the intricacies of the role. Focus your marking scheme around the skills that all the candidates have demonstrated rather than their insights into the role you are trying to fill.

If all the candidates for the position are internal, it would be foolish in the extreme to ignore all the insights that the organisation already has of the candidates. While an interview will help you to compare and contrast the applicants, you should avoid basing your decision on the interview alone; you should consider taking track record, performance evaluations and how the organisation values their contribution into consideration also. Decide then what proportion of your rating will be allocated to performance appraisal review scores and supervisor reports, taking account of any internal promotion policies. Supervisor reports will only be useful to you if they are of a high standard, objective and consistent across the organisation.

What the pros say: ✓

- One meeting with a candidate is not enough on which to base your decision.
- Never make a selection single-handedly.
- Work at developing and building rapport with other interviewers; you need to work together as a team.
- Nobody has a monopoly on insights, so take notice of other interviewers' views, especially when they are based on hard evidence.
- Interviewing and making hiring decisions takes time: always err on the generous side in planning and scheduling the time it will take.
- Don't look on the time you spend as a nuisance: getting the right person to fill a vacancy is a significant part of any manager's role, and being a good interviewer is an integral part of any manager's skill set.

The lazy interviewer: ✗

- Doesn't change their interview approach over time and is likely to have interviewed the same way for years
- Relies on one interview – claiming they 'just know' who the best candidate is
- Considers all the other methods of selection a waste of time
- Is not prepared to put time into anything except the single interview
- Pays no attention to suggestions from other interviewers

The best interviewers: ✓

- Put time into planning and preparation, and allow enough time to do a thorough job
- Impose structure on the interview
- Take control of the interview process to ensure it runs smoothly
- Make hiring decisions on the basis of more than one encounter with the candidate
- See candidates from as many angles as possible
- Realise that they are part of a team in making selection decisions
- Ensure that the insights of all involved are included in the mix

Coaches' Corner – Things for You to Try

- Network with colleagues to find out what has or hasn't worked for them in recent recruitment campaigns.
- Try out different types of interviews.
- Vary your interview formula: don't get locked into one way of conducting an interview.

5

Getting the Chemistry Right

Provoking Question

- *Have you ever wondered whether you could have done anything more to give that nervous interviewee a chance to settle down and shine at the interview?*

In this chapter you will learn how to:

- Create the right interview atmosphere
- Build rapport with candidates
- Deal with different personality types
- Sharpen your listening skills
- Take good notes

Real-life Experience

Derek and Helen had never worked together before but spent two days interviewing together for a couple of new test engineers. Helen knew less than Derek about the area and deferred to his judgement because of that.

However, she felt that he was quick to jump to conclusions about candidates, and he had a particular disregard for any interviewee who was a bit nervous, arguing that they wouldn't be able to handle the heat in the kitchen! He liked to apply a bit of pressure to see how candidates would respond, and Helen was a bit uneasy about this as a tactic. Between them both, she felt they hadn't created the right climate to allow the interviewees to be their real selves.

As well as doing the interviewees a grave disservice, Derek and Helen's lack of rapport was probably very obvious to the interviewees – and not conducive to helping them relax and perform well at the interview.

The biggest challenge facing interviewers such as Derek and Helen is how to get a fair and accurate assessment of an interviewee from the interview and other selection tools. The best way of meeting that challenge is by making the interview as close to a real-life, meaningful interaction as possible. When the interviewer actively creates a climate of open communication, the interviewee will feel at ease, the mask will gradually slip, and the interviewee will settle into revealing more of their true self.

Creating the Right Atmosphere

From the very first contact your organisation has with a candidate through the advertising process, you can influence what their relationship with you will be like. The tone of the advert and the way the candidate is contacted and dealt with in advance of the interview, right down to what information they get in advance about the job and the selection process, together with the arrangements for the interview and the physical location of the interview, can all have an impact on whether the candidate feels respected.

Before the Interview

There are some steps you can take to create a welcoming environment before candidates step into the interview room, as follows:

- Have a comfortable waiting area with an appropriate level of privacy, where candidates will not have to meet with their competitors or staff who may know them personally.
- Have someone briefed to expect the candidate and be available to steer them in the right direction – a pleasant, welcoming face will help the candidate to relax and perform better at the start of the interview.
- One of the interviewers should be primed to make the first approach, to bring the candidate from the waiting area into the interview room and to exchange a few lines of pleasantries to relax the candidate on the way, rather than walking along together in stern silence.

Room Layout

Comfort and an air of congeniality will help interviewees to relax and be their normal selves. The following guidelines will help you create a relaxing space:

- A round table rather than a straight one ensures a more relaxed vibe. If there are more than two of you interviewing together, or if you don't have a round table, congregate around one corner of the table so that you don't take on the appearance of an interrogation committee sitting in a long row.
- Test out the interviewee chair for distance from the interviewers: being too close is as uncomfortable as being too far away. There is an optimum distance that will depend on the size of the table and how many interviewers there are.
- Make sure the chair doesn't squeak or make noises as the poor interviewee squirms on it, and ensure it is set at an appropriate height. Don't keep the 'good' chairs for the interviewers and leave the wrecked, cast-off chair with the wobbly legs for the interviewee!
- Don't have light from a window facing directly into the interviewee's face, as they will then find it hard to see you clearly.
- Take control of the space and use it wisely – don't be a slave to the way the room is already laid out.
- Have a glass of water near the interviewee and a copy of their CV or application for them to have a look at, rather than having all the paper on your side of the table.
- Keep your own paperwork neat and clutter free; it can be a bit disconcerting for the interviewee to see a huge pile of applications on the desk, and it gives the impression that this interviewee is only a number. Put everything to one side, off the table, keeping only what you need for this one interview in front of you.
- Never let the interviewee see the names or CVs of other candidates.

- Use name cards to identify the interviewers in formal board-type interviews.
- Make sure the room is at optimum temperature: the interviewee will be on the 'hot seat', so allow for that. Also, you don't want to get too warm yourself, as it will make it more difficult to concentrate. Keep an eye on this if you are interviewing throughout the day and make adjustments to the room temperature if you need to.
- If possible, have a wall clock in sight of the interviewers.

Introductions

The first few minutes of the interview set a clear marker for how the atmosphere will progress. Most interviewers with any bit of common sense and good manners will make introductions and invite the candidate to sit comfortably and relax. This is what the candidate expects, and it provides a moment for all to settle down. Arrange beforehand how you will manage the handshaking: do you move around to greet the candidate as you are being introduced or do you introduce yourself as you shake hands? Interviewees also like to know who is who, although in many cases they will have been told in advance who they will meet on the day. They also like to place people in context: the guy on the left is the technical guru who will ask me specialist questions, or the person on the right is from HR and will probably ask me questions about my personality and attitude! While you need to explain, don't overdo it either; the candidate recognises that this is a preamble and will want to get on with the interview proper, whether they are nervous or not.

Building Rapport

Your goal as an interviewer is to feel that you have connected with the interviewee and that they have engaged with you in a meaningful dialogue. To reach this goal there are a number of useful techniques that involve both your verbal and non-verbal behaviour, as follows:

- Use the candidate's first name frequently, but check first what they like to be called, as the name on their CV may be their more formal name.
- Smile – do it naturally and frequently.
- Use your eyes to connect – look the interviewee in the eye, even when another interviewer is talking. Your eyebrows can also help to show you're interested and listening when you raise them slightly. However, be aware that different nationalities have different preferences on eye contact and stance.
- Engage positively – lean forward slightly in your seat. This will help you concentrate, as well as show that you are listening, and it will encourage the interviewee to speak.
- Small sounds of agreement and encouragement can settle a candidate who is nervous.

Adapting to a Candidate's Verbal and Non-verbal Behaviour

Not all communication takes place through verbal content. The message from sender to receiver passes through the prism of non-verbal behaviour. Body language includes all aspects of eye contact, facial expression and body movement that add to the impact of what is being said and influence how the 'message' is picked up and interpreted by the receiver. Voice quality, volume, pitch, speed and other aspects of voice can also give you clues about the attitude of the speaker. For the interviewer, the ability to pick up on aspects of non-verbal behaviour is crucial. For instance, if the content of what the interviewee is saying doesn't match their general body language, the non-verbal behaviour may give a truer picture of the person's feelings – but you will need to probe further to be really sure, as the following case studies demonstrate:

Case Study 1: Visual Clues

Fraser is an experienced interviewer: when he is asking a question, he does not look down at his papers but focuses on the candidate's facial reactions, which can indicate if the candidate is feeling nervous or confident, comfortable or uncomfortable.

Case Study 2: Listen to the Music

Jill has been interviewing clerical staff for over ten years. In her experience, she can hear from changes in voice inflexion if an answer is weak. For example, if somebody is claiming someone else's work as their own, she notices that the tone of their voice changes, and they may begin to move around in their seat. But she doesn't rely on her gut instincts. She uses it as an opportunity to probe and get hard information to ensure the reliability of the answers she is getting.

Dealing with Nervous Candidates

Being interviewed for a job can be a very daunting experience, even for people who are normally self-confident. Some interviewees can mask the tension they feel more than others. Watch out for the warning signs, such as sweating, trembling hands, dry mouth, neck or face rash, and hesitant or trembling voice tone, as these will tell you that you need to put more effort into building rapport and relaxing the candidate. At the less dramatic extreme, you will also notice candidates who lose track of what they were going to say due to nervousness. To reduce nervousness:

- Get the candidate talking about areas that they are especially good at and ease back on the deep probing until they have had a chance to get talking about some areas of their expertise that show them in a good light.
- Continue to make eye contact, with a gentle, expectant facial expression, even though the candidate may find it hard to engage you with direct eye contact in return.
- If the candidate still looks nervous, reassure them that the interview is not an interrogation, that they should take a drink, sit back and try to relax. Acknowledge that you understand that many interviewees will be a bit nervous and that you will do your best to make the interview as pleasant an experience as possible.

Bear in mind that not all jobs require extroverts, so do not unnecessarily mark a quiet candidate down; they may be just what you need in terms of their consistency, reliability and ability to quietly get the job done. You do not need all your employees to be centre-stage characters. Check references carefully and consider giving a second interview in a more relaxed setting, over a cup of coffee, for instance, if you feel a candidate has potential that you could not uncover due to their nervousness.

Dealing with Candidates Who Are Overly Talkative

The agenda for the interview and the management of time are the responsibility of the interviewers. Many candidates misunderstand what the appropriate level of detail of their responses should be; sometimes this is due to nervousness, but it can also be a warning sign that they are not the best of communicators. To recover control:

- Pull back on the rapport-building techniques and reduce your level of eye contact.
- Use certain front-end phrases to indicate that you want short answers. For instance, begin questions with phrases such as:
  - 'Very briefly could you tell me ...'
  - 'In three short sentences could you tell me exactly what your role was in ...'
  - 'We're running short on time now, and I'm concerned that I'm not getting the exact details about you that I need. Can you help me out by keeping your answers short and to the point, and I'll try to keep my questions very specific?'
- In other words, intervene graciously, but get the message across that you want less detail, less painting of context, or less superlatives in the interviewee's descriptions of themself or whatever it is that's causing the interview to derail.

Normally, we would advise not to interrupt an interviewee, but if the candidate is running away with the interview you may have to take control by intervening in a very direct way. More serious challenging techniques are covered in Chapter 8.

Dealing with an Interviewee Who Is Not Forthcoming

Sometimes, despite your best efforts, you cannot get the interviewee to expand on their answers or give a full and accurate account of what they have done and what they will bring to the job. In such circumstances, look again at their CV and see whether they have shown evidence of working alongside other people or if they have played a key role in teams.

What do they do in their spare time? Do they spend time in the company of friends, and do they get engaged and enthusiastic about anything at all? You should probe those elements of the CV to see if you can establish what type of team player they have been and what their level of social interaction is. You may begin to see a pattern emerging of more solitary behaviour than you might want.

If you have genuinely tried all of the techniques advised earlier, then you can do no more. The interviewee has to meet you half-way.

Dealing with an Interviewee Who Is Clearly Not Suitable

Many interviewers tend to make up their minds about candidates far too early in the interview process. However, even when you suspend judgement and use good, sharp questioning techniques, it can be apparent from early on that some candidates are way short of what you are looking for.

Should you just cut such interviews short rather than waste the time of the candidate and put them through the wringer unnecessarily?

It is advisable to cover the main areas of your spec for two reasons: you want to show that all interviewees got the same treatment and, also, you do not want the interviewee to feel they didn't get a good chance to tell their story. This is especially true when interviewing for internal promotions, where candidates will compare notes afterwards.

Also, bear in mind that the interviewee is likely to have spent considerable time preparing their application and presenting for interview, perhaps taking leave from work and going to expense to get to the interview. They deserve some of your time in return. If the interview has been a one-off, informal interview of a single candidate, you can be a bit more pragmatic: ask the candidate what they think about their match with the job, and what skill or experience gaps they have. You can explain that you were looking for something a bit different than what they have to offer.

Some interviewees are slow bloomers and take time to blossom at interview: allow the more reserved candidate the time to settle down and become comfortable.

Stress Interviewing

The interview is like no other interaction for the interviewee. As interviewer, you have received an amount of personal detail about them on their CV: you know how they got on at school or university, where they work, what their work achievements have or haven't been, what they do in their spare time, etc. You are about to put them through their paces and – as they perceive it – try to pick holes in their competence. Their future may take a significant turn if they are offered a job with you. All of this makes the interviewee feel exposed.

Some interviewers believe the best way to test whether someone can handle the pressure of the job they are hiring for is to deliberately inject stress into the interview. There is no evidence that the pressure felt at interview is similar to normal job-related pressure. On the contrary, it may send out a very negative message about the company's culture and may put off desirable candidates. It is better as an interviewer to get on with asking good, probing questions that examine how the candidate dealt with deadlines and pressures in the past, rather than taking on the 'bad cop' facade. There will be quite enough challenge in the interview if you are asking probing, searching questions.

Role of Humour in Interviewing

The interview is a serious meeting. Interviewers and interviewees have business to get through, and interviewees expect it to be a fairly formal process. The challenge for you as interviewer is to get through the agenda in a business-like way while keeping the interview friendly and relaxed. If a small touch of humour helps to keep that balance right, then go with it. However, being naturally pleasant is often a better bet, as humour can cause the nervous interviewee to become more nervous still.

Listening Skills

We ask questions to steer the conversation towards our agenda, but it is through listening actively and carefully that we collect material which we can use to evaluate each candidate. Active listening is no easy job; when you examine the following list, you begin to understand that it demands both energy and concentration:

Listening for fact: this involves listening accurately for the facts, but also for exaggerations, generic statements, vagueness and non sequiturs that get in the way of establishing the real facts.

Listening for feeling behind facts: for example, discomfort, lack of confidence, pressure, disappointment, frustration, cynicism, egotism, etc.

Listen for what's not said: listen out for what the candidate chooses not to include in a description of an experience or for the way the candidate tries to steer you away from their zone of discomfort.

Listen for 'throwaway' comments: these may not be related to what has been asked but can be very telling. For example, the candidate is giving an account of a project they managed and, as a 'by the way' to a description of how they handled it, they mention a team member and say, 'They were always a bit of a moan anyway.' Now you get the sense that maybe the interviewee lacks the ability to empathise or to deal with complaints, and could be a bit too ready to judge harshly.

Listening beyond your remit: you may be interviewing with others and have carved up the questions between you. Although you may be asking about one area, you may get information back about another area of the spec – interviewees will not be compartmentalising their answers to suit your game plan!

Listening through silence: when you ask a searching question, wait for the interviewee to ponder their answer without jumping in to rescue them. If the question was tough and challenging, it's only right to give the candidate the chance to think through and formulate an answer.

Listening with energy: one of the biggest challenges for interviewers is that of staying focussed and energetic. More than anything, a genuine interest in the candidate in front of you will keep you focussed, so lean forward, look them straight in the eye and stay with it!

Listening for logic: does the candidate take you through what they want to say in a step-by-step way that is easy to understand; do they break down the answer into component parts and see all the angles?

Listening for the ego: when talking about their background and achievements, does the candidate show a realistic view of themselves and their strengths and weaknesses? Do they acknowledge the contribution of others, and can they see their own flaws?

Listening for attitude: if you ask the candidate what went wrong, are they quick to blame others rather than tell you what they learned from their mistakes? Enthusiasm is another example of an attitude that can help you differentiate between candidates – an enthusiastic candidate positively invites you to probe their experience! Just be sure to check that the enthusiasm is genuine.

Note-taking

Taking notes is a necessary part of interviewing. The real trick in note-taking is to minimise the amount of notes you have to take. You should avoid the following:

- Notes that repeat information presented elsewhere in the application form, CV or letter of application
- Concentrating on writing and ignoring the speaker
- Taking too many notes – aim for one page per interviewee
- Writing down full sentences, which will make it difficult to keep up with the interviewee

You need notes as reminders, prompts, summaries and to jot down evidence to help in your post-interview assessment. However, taking notes can get in the way of good two-way communication and can be a distraction to the candidate. Interviewees are often thrown off course by the interviewers' note-taking, as they assume it is some evidence against them that is being taking down in true policeman fashion.

The following are some hints as to how you can interview *and* take some notes at the same time:

- Let the interviewee know that you will be taking notes and that you may ask them to repeat key information so that you can record it.
- Use a pro forma interview recording sheet laid out in tabular form, as shown below, with headings for the competencies and the information or 'evidence' you get from the candidate so that you can record the information you have gleaned during the interview.

Pro Forma Interview Recording Sheet

Competency	Evidence	Mark Out of 100
Leadership	Chaired office c'ttee 2 yrs; saw need for change, got team views, had plan, target met. Helped underperformer improve delivery. Etc.	85

- Use keywords, phrases and abbreviations.
- Record numbers and other relevant proofs.
- When you have finished interviewing and pass to another interviewer, write down what is in your mind.
- New information which has not been provided elsewhere by the candidate must be recorded.
- Do not allow your note-taking to get in the way of the interview or to be a distraction to the candidate. Be unobtrusive in the way you take notes so that you focus on what's being said and maintain rapport at all times.

- It *is* possible to listen and write at the same time, but don't look at what you are writing. With a little practice you can develop the skill of writing minimal notes without looking at them – although you won't win any prizes for calligraphy! Keep up your eye contact with the candidate while jotting down what you need to remember.
- Use the time between interviews to check over your notes.

It is common practice for interviewers in formal public service interviews to submit their notes to the chairperson so that the key points supporting the marking can be recorded on a master sheet. See also Chapter 9 for legal implications and guidelines for taking interview notes.

What the pros say: ✓

- The niceties of politeness should not be an empty ritual: engage in a meaningful way with each candidate rather than going through the motions.
- The first few minutes of the interview are crucial for setting the right atmosphere.
- Be brutal with time but gracious with people.
- The best test of a good interview is if the interviewee feels they have been put through their paces and have had to think on their feet some of the time to respond to searching questions.
- Playing 'good cop, bad cop' can be counterproductive.
- Good note-taking is a balance between recording as much as possible (for legal reasons) and as little as possible (to ensure proper rapport with the interviewee).

The lazy interviewer: ✕

- Doesn't bother to make the effort to connect with each candidate
- Takes no time beforehand to set up a good interview environment
- Uses the same approach with all candidates no matter what their personality type
- Makes no effort to stay focussed and loses interest – appears lethargic and distracted
- Ignores the non-verbal signals, such as shifting eye contact, changes in voice, emphasis, tone and body language

The best interviewers:

- Show a natural respect for, and interest in, all candidates, whether they are suitable or not
- Naturally put people at ease
- Listen more than they talk, operating the 80/20 rule
- Pick up nuances of personality and attitude from candidate's verbal and non-verbal behaviour
- Know how to engage the interviewee naturally but also how to interrupt and re-direct them when necessary

Coaches' Corner – Things for You to Try

- Have a few introductory lines and pleasantries up your sleeve for those first few words when you meet a candidate – don't always rely on the usual suspects of weather or traffic congestion!
- Start to become conscious of what impression you give to people on first meeting them: study your facial expressions in a mirror and ask yourself whether people would open up to you.
- Walk around between interviews, open the window, take a stretch, take a few deep breaths, grab a cup of coffee or a glass of water, change seats with other interviewers – whatever it takes to stay energised!
- Practice some of the rapport-building skills discussed in this chapter in any social interaction, especially when meeting someone for the first time.
- Practice taking notes without looking at them, at the same time as you're talking or listening at meetings.

6

Asking the Right Questions to Get the Best Candidate

Provoking Question

- *Just because the interviewee answered the question are you sure you got what you were looking for?*

In this chapter you will learn how to:

- Expand your repertoire of interview questions
- Ask good questions
- Probe more deeply
- Probe a candidate's education and technical expertise

Real-life Experience

Hilary had done it by the book: she had put a good job specification together and had done an in-depth competency profile for the new sales manager role. She had asked her colleagues what interview questions had worked well for them in the past, and they had supplied her with a list. During the interview things seemed to flow well, and she had all the right boxes ticked. Yet, when the interviews were over, she had two problems. The first was that it had all been a bit too easy: she had got the right answers first time, and most of the candidates had done equally well. How was she going to pick the best one? The other problem she had was a vague feeling that somehow or other she had missed the point of the interview process, which was to identify the best candidate and rank the rest.

Now what was she going to do? Having spent all that time interviewing, she could hardly say she hadn't made up her mind, and yet she couldn't offer the job to any of the candidates in complete confidence that she was making the right decision. Would her decision to hire hold water? She would have to keep her fingers crossed and hope it would work out okay ...

To make the right choice of candidate the interviewer must not only get the right answers, they must probe to ensure that the answers they are getting reflect the real-life experiences of the interviewee. Hilary may have been content to tick off the answers to the standard questions on her list, but how can she be sure she got the deepest insights into each candidate if she didn't dig a little deeper? A common flaw is for interviewers to relax and let their guard down once they have got the interviewee talking. Instead, they need to stay in the driver's seat and steer the interview towards the realities of what exactly this candidate has to offer.

The Power of Questions

We have come to rely on the interview as the favoured method of engaging with job applicants and pitting one candidate against another so we can rank them. It can be a rich exchange, where the interviewers and interviewee engage in a meaningful and robust discussion about the candidate's suitability for the job. But this level of dialogue requires a mastery of a wide range of questioning techniques to steer the conversation. The art of good questioning is key to moving the interview from a pedestrian ritual of question and answer to a more fundamental level of communication that goes way beyond trite questions and pat answers.

Questions: An Open and Shut Case?

Questions can be categorised along a spectrum from closed to open, as follows:

- The most closed form of question invites a 'yes' or 'no' answer: 'You started work there two years ago; is that right?'
- A less closed form looks for a specific piece of information: 'What year did you start there?'
- A slightly more open version would be: 'What was your role there?' or 'What were the main challenges for you in that job?'
- At the more extreme end of the spectrum, a very open question would be: 'Tell me about your last job.'

Interviewers who tend to be too loose in framing open questions get poor results: when asked how he found America,

John Lennon famously replied, 'First turn left after Greenland!' The skilled interviewer will be able to formulate questions for all points on the continuum.

Asking Good Questions

The standard cliché in interviewing is to encourage interviewers to ask the six standard questions: who, what, when, where, how and why? However, to get full value out of them you will need to use them properly.

Who, what, when and where are *information-gathering* questions; they will give you the basic facts. Use them to establish the essentials of time and place, as follows:

*   *When* was that?
*   *Who* else was involved?
*   *Where* did you work before that?
*   *What* exactly was your role there?

How and why are *probing* questions and can help you get deeper into the candidate's motivations and behaviour, which is exactly where you want to get to. Examples of probing questions include the following:

*   *How* did you go about that?
*   *How* did you come to that conclusion?
*   *How* did you feel about that?

'Why' is useful as a probe in understanding peoples' motivation for doing something. For example:

- *Why* did you decide to do it that way?
- *Why* did you think that was more important?
- *Why* did you move jobs from Company A to Company B?

Sometimes interviewees do not respond well to a question beginning with why, as they see it as challenging their thinking or actions. The skilled interviewer may need to reframe the question to get the right effect. For example, instead of asking, 'Why did you do it that way?' which might sound like you don't agree with how the interviewee dealt with something, the interviewer could ask, 'What factors did you take into account when you decided to do it that way?'

It can be helpful to soften your questions by using a front-end phrase or statement to qualify them, such as, 'I'd like to ask you about managing teams: how would you describe your leadership style?'

Questions can be asked to give the applicant the chance to say what they did well, but they can also be phrased so as to find out what went wrong. Sometimes we learn more about the candidate from the difficulties they struggled with and how they fixed the problem. For example:

Interviewer: 'Did any problems occur when the system went live?'
Interviewee: 'It mostly went according to plan, but some of the branches were unable to access the information immediately.'
Interviewer: 'How did you deal with that?'

The trick is to use the investigative reporter's technique: stay on the case! Investigative journalists are used to interviewees dodging their questions because they do not want to implicate themselves. But journalists are outcome-driven, i.e. they know the information they have to come away with for the interview to be successful, so they ask the same questions in different ways.

Questions That Are Not What They Seem

One basic problem with communication is that, while the message may seem perfectly clear to the sender, it can mean something different to the receiver. Interviewers may ask questions in too general a form, and the interviewee may find it difficult, if not impossible, to understand the intention of the questions asked.

'Tell Me About' Questions

To get an interviewee talking, a standard interviewing technique is to ask for information in a generalised, 'tell me about' (or similar) format, such as the following:

- Tell me about yourself.
- Tell me about your last job.
- Take me through your CV.

This type of question encourages the interviewee to talk. Well-prepared interviewees will generally supply what you need in a concise and logical way and, for this reason, it is generally a very useful type of question. However, when interviewers ask too many loose questions the interviewee is conditioned to give only long and loose answers; it then becomes virtually impossible for them to give short, concise answers. The danger of using 'tell me about' questions repeatedly is that the interviewee will waffle.

When 'Tell Me About' Is Not Helpful

How do you know the question you use will get you the information you want? What can happen is that the interviewer asks one question but the interviewee answers another, as follows:

Interviewer: 'Tell me about your experience as a manager.'

Interviewee: 'When I moved to my last job I was given a managerial role for the first time. I enjoyed it and didn't really have any problems with it, and it was a great company to work for.'

The general form of the question gives a very general answer, so we get little idea of what their management style is like. The following, more specific question would be better:

Interviewer: 'What sort of things did you do to help staff perform better?'

Interviewee: 'I set targets quarterly and monthly but kept informal contact going day to day.'

Leading Questions and the Oblique Approach

If you lead too much with your question you may get a bland answer. For instance, you want to know how well the interviewee handles pressure and you ask a leading question, as follows:

> **Interviewer:** 'How do you normally handle pressure at work?'
> **Interviewee:** 'I can handle it very well; I never get stressed really.'

The interviewer has put the interviewee on alert; the interviewee now knows the interviewer is looking for someone who can handle pressure well and so is prompted to give a generalised answer that apparently shows them in a very positive light but gives little true insight into how they would behave in a given situation. Sometimes you will have to go around the subject rather than tackle it head on, as in the following questions:

- 'You mentioned that those types of projects are run to very tight deadlines; presumably that puts pressure on everyone. What was the worst example of a very tight deadline that you had on one of those projects?'
- 'How did people generally respond to that level of pressure?'
- 'What was the hardest part of that pressure for you personally?'
- 'If you had a similar project with such a tight deadline in the future, would you cope any differently with it?'

By acknowledging directly that such a situation is bound to be highly pressured you are not giving the interviewee room to wriggle out of the question by claiming that everything went without a hitch.

Get More In: Use a Funnel!

You can get more into a container and get it in more quickly if you use a funnel. As an interviewer, you can get more information from candidates by using a funnelling type sequence of questions, whereby you move from broad inquiries to more specific questions, as follows:

1. **Headline the area you are about to explore:** 'I would like you to tell us about your experience of leading teams.'
2. **Start with open questions:** 'What are the main types of situation in which you have had to assume leadership of your team?'
3. **Focus the conversation with moderately open questions:** 'Which situations would be most relevant to this job?'
4. **Switch to a closed question:** 'Can we focus on the last one you mentioned?'
5. **Switch back to a moderately open question:** 'What were the main things you did to manage the situation?'

6. **Follow with supplementary open questions** to get full details of exactly what the candidate did in the situation, what approach they took, how it worked out, etc.
7. **Use summaries to check that you have the right information:** 'So you are telling me that …'
8. **End with a closed question:** 'Have I got that right?' or 'Is there anything else you would like to add?'

The problem with prepared questions is that you cannot anticipate beforehand what the candidate's answers are going to be, so you will not be in a position to plan your follow-up questions in advance. You need to keep the conversation going in a definite direction until you have a clear idea of what the candidate has done and what situations they have experienced, in order to get a sense of what type of person they are. You want to know:

- What they have done
- How they get the job done and how they have responded to various situations
- How well they can transfer that experience to the job you want them to do

Probing a Candidate's Education

It is not sufficient to take good qualifications at face value. If a candidate claims they have a good degree or certificate, the temptation is to ask them questions to test their knowledge. This turns the interview into some form of *Mastermind* competition. It is not a question of probing what they can remember but discovering how they learn and how they manage themselves and apply their learning. You also need to take account of levels of experience. For example, if you are interviewing a recent graduate who has very limited work experience, the following are some useful questions:

- What would you say the college experience was like for you?
- Which subject presented the greatest challenges for you?
- How did you organise yourself to master the subject?
- How did you manage your time at college?
- How did you manage exam stress and pressure?
- We all manage our study in different ways; which worked better for you: study groups or individual work?
- Did your college experience give you any insights as to what type of job would suit you best?
- In what ways did you change as a person during your years at college?
- Is there anything you regret about your years at university?

You would adopt a different approach to a candidate who, for example, chose to do an MBA mid-career, as follows:

- How did you select your particular MBA?
- What gaps in knowledge/skills did you hope to fill when you decided to do the MBA?
- What new knowledge did this course give you?
- What did you learn about yourself through the course?
- How did your study groups help you? What kind of frustrations did you have to deal with when working with other students? How did you deal with them?

- Are you approaching your work any differently since finishing the course?
- What benefits do you think your employer and colleagues have seen?

Probing a Candidate's Technical Expertise

How do you know the candidate is expert in their field? To find out, you can:

- Look at qualifications and see if they got a good result.
- Pose some technical questions that would test their level of expertise – you could either paint a scenario or a number of scenarios where they would have to use their knowledge to solve a problem or ask them to describe in detail how they approached some tricky technical problems in the past. It is important to ask lots of follow-up questions to ensure the candidate has the level and depth of knowledge you need.
- Have a separate technical interview that is knowledge-based and asks a number of searching questions that test the candidate's knowledge.
- Give a written test.

What the pros say: ✓

- The way you shape a question has a direct impact on the type of information you get back.
- Good interviewers use a wide repertoire of different types of questions.

- Leading questions are not helpful: get at information more obliquely by asking who, what, when, where, how and why questions.
- Focus on getting the right outcome: avoid stock questions – have alternatives available that look for the same information.
- Take time to drill deep into each area of the candidate's expertise with your questions rather than hop from one topic to another.
- Good interviewers hear everything that is said and *how* it is said.

The lazy interviewer:

- Uses their standard or favourite questions
- Does not probe
- Compiles a list of challenging questions and looks for the 'right' answer, reducing the interview to the level of a quiz
- Goes into autopilot – loses track of the interview and the interviewee
- Ticks off the boxes if they get anything sounding vaguely like the right answer
- Scores on a narrow basis and is only interested in yes or no type answers
- Asks leading questions that suggest the correct answers

The best interviewers:

- Probe, probe, probe – until they hit bedrock!
- Ask clear questions
- Are clear about the exact information they are looking for
- Are conscious of shaping and framing questions to suit what they want to find out
- Show versatility in their choice of questions rather than using a jaded list of favourites
- Are driven by a need to be convinced of the quality of the interviewee's answers
- Act like investigative journalists to get at the real facts

Coaches' Corner – Things for You to Try

- Move outside your comfort zone! Most interviewers rely on a limited set of favourite questions that have worked well for them in the past.
- Explore the power of all six basic question types.
- Listen to interviewers on TV and radio and see what types of questions they ask and what questions work best for them.
- Practice summarising and reflecting back in your normal conversations with people.
- Find colleagues to test your skills with. Practice some of your questions on colleagues so that you can be sure of the range of answers you are going to get.

7

Getting the Full Story: Competency-based Interviewing

Provoking Questions

- *How can you be certain that the candidate who seems to be steaming into first place really has the skills and knowledge to deliver on the ground if offered the job?*
- *Is competency–based interviewing a good approach to take?*

In this chapter you will learn how to:

- Define competencies
- Use a competency-based framework of questions
- Ensure you don't take what is said at face value
- Recognise and deal with candidates' exaggerations

Real-life Experience

Kirsten and Tony had spent two full days interviewing ten candidates. They had gone through their list of prepared questions with each of the candidates and had a front-runner who was marginally ahead of the others, but when they talked it through afterwards they weren't really clear on why this person was better than the others. Many of his answers were polished: they got a lot of information about the various roles he had been in, the types of companies he had worked for, and his views on many aspects of technology development and people management. All of this seemed faultless. Yet they had a lingering feeling that they did not know him fully, and they therefore couldn't be certain that he would deliver the goods in the challenging role they wanted to fill. What could they have done differently, they wondered? Did their questions allow them to cut to the heart of the matter?

Kirsten and Tony need to guarantee that they have an accurate picture of the front-runner's skills and expertise and greater certainty that he will deliver on the job. How can they be certain that he is the best of the bunch? In Chapter 6 we looked at the power of questions and how to frame questions to probe deeply and get the information you want. You want to get the full picture, including a sense of who the person really is. You also want to get a sense of what level of skill and competency they have. In short, you want to know whether the candidate has what it takes to do a really good job.

Introduction to Competency-based Interviewing

As an interviewer, you are faced with endless choices of questions to ask a candidate. The challenge is to use the interview time productively to get the maximum insight in the shortest period. Over the years, recruitment practitioners have developed the interview into a more refined and objective exercise in an attempt to get the most out of the interview process. The practice of giving structured, planned interviews where candidates are measured against preset criteria is now common. A refinement to the process that has gained widespread support is the competency-based approach to interviewing. This approach is now a common practice in many organisations. It is also the preferred practice in public sector bodies. It is not without its serious critics, however, and we will look at how you can take the best aspects of the approach and insert them into your range of interviewing skills and strategies.

> Competency-based interviewing is based on the premise that *the best predictor of future performance is past performance and past behaviour*.

How Does It Work?

With competency-based interviewing each candidate is measured against a list of competencies that are especially relevant to the job on offer. The interviewers then have a set of ratings for each candidate at the end of the interviews. Normally when using the competency approach, the interviewers follow a preset framework of questions. The framework tends to operate like this:

1. The interviewer chooses one of the competencies they want the successful candidate to have.

2. The interviewer asks the interviewee for an example of a situation which exemplifies that competence and gets some background information to put the example in context.
3. When the interviewee chooses their example, the interviewer asks them questions to examine exactly:
    ○ *What* the candidate did
    ○ *How* they went about it, e.g. what alternative actions they may have considered
    ○ *What* the outcome was – in clear, specific terms
    They may also ask, 'What did you *learn* from that experience?'

What Do We Mean by a Competency?

A competency is a skill, a set of knowledge or expertise, or a personal quality needed to do a job well. As an interviewer, you will need to examine the job in its entirety and decide what the job holder will need to do it well. In Chapter 2 we outlined this for shortlisting purposes.

You will find that some competencies are common to nearly all jobs, e.g. drive/energy, while some will be very job-specific, e.g. technical product knowledge. The list you draw up should range across skills, knowledge and personal qualities, as follows:

Skill-based competency: while the classic example of a skill would be craft skills, such as carpentry or plumbing, there are as many skills as there are jobs, e.g. keyboard skills, forklift driving, numeracy, ability to write advanced programmes in Java, analytical/problem-solving skills, report writing, etc.

Knowledge-based competency: this is what you need to know to do the job, such as knowledge of competitors' products, statistics, legislation or legal precedents relevant to the business.

Trait-type competency: this relates to the inherent attitudes, motivation, confidence and elements of disposition that affect how someone behaves and interacts both with the job and with other people. An example would be the ability to handle pressure and deadlines calmly and be prepared to make whatever personal efforts are needed under these work conditions to get tasks done well and on time. Another example would be the ability to accept feedback constructively. A trait is the sum of an individual's nature and nurture, and can run deep and be less amenable to change than either skills or knowledge. It is vital that your chosen candidate has the appropriate personal attributes to interface well with the job and those with whom they interact.

How Many Competencies Do I Need to Look For?

The number of competencies you choose to use should be manageable – not more than about five in number, with each one separate and distinct from the others. You can group a number of linked competencies under one general heading. This then forms the basis for a marking scheme which you can use to rate all candidates.

A simple competency framework for a customer care team leader might look as follows:

Simple Competency Framework
• **Knowledge:** of company products and procedures, motivation techniques and consumer rights
• **Skills:** supervising staff, deciding on disputes, escalating complaints, problem solving, organising, etc.
• **Traits:** patience, persistence, confidence and self-motivation

Using a Competency-based Framework of Questions

In the simplest version of a competency-based interview the interviewer will ask the interviewee for one or more examples of how they demonstrated their competencies in previous positions, using such questions as, 'Can you give me an example of when you showed you had good problem-solving skills?' or 'Tell be about a time when you had to resolve a conflict with a colleague.' The difficulty with these questions is that the interviewee will take a 'one I prepared earlier' approach, which leads you into rehearsed territory where the interviewee is in the driving seat. To get better traction, the interviewer will have to impose a more sophisticated structure and sequence on their questions. The structure can be easily remembered by the acronym EARL, as follows:

*E*xperience
*A*ctions taken to reach result
*R*esults or outcomes of effort
*L*earning from this experience and applying that knowledge in future

Experience

The interviewers want to establish whether the interviewee has first-hand experience of certain situations or has had an opportunity to demonstrate a particular skill. They can then probe the interviewee's examples in detail to get a real sense of their calibre, as follows:

> **Interviewer:** 'Leading teams is an essential part of this job; can you give me an idea of the types of teams you have led?'

The interviewer then chooses one example from the response that they want the interviewee to focus on, as follows:

> **Interviewer:** 'This job requires experience in leading a project-based team to deal with queries from customers following a product launch roll-out. Can you tell me more about your experience in managing that project-based team you mentioned just now?'
> **Interviewee:** (Supplies details.)
> **Interviewer:** 'What were you trying to achieve?'
> **Interviewee:** 'We wanted to reduce the backlog to one day for 90 per cent of cases, with the rest to be cleared by the weekend.'

Actions

The interviewer wants to know exactly what the interviewee did in a given situation in order to establish their range of skills. They may also want to find out the range of options that were considered, rejected or accepted, and the reasons why. This will give valuable insight into the applicant's ability to analyse a situation and make judgement calls, as follows:

> **Interviewer:** 'What approach did you take?'
> **Interviewee:** 'Firstly, I analysed the backlog cases and classified them …'
> **Interviewer:** 'What problems did you encounter and how did you overcome them? Did you get the team to pull out all the stops for you? How?'

Results

Actions without quantifiable results are useless to the interviewer as proof that the applicant acted effectively in a particular situation. A common error is for interviewers to get long lists of actions without any indication of their impact. The interviewer is looking for the outcomes, results and metrics that were achieved and also needs to establish that the outcomes were of a calibre that matches the level of the job. To prove that the actions had impact, you could ask specific questions, such as the following:

- What scale of improvements resulted?
- What measures of success did you use?
- How much of the result was directly attributable to you alone?
- How did your results compare with targets?

Learning

The best performers learn on the job and never stop learning, and the smartest people also make mistakes – but they learn from them. The interviewer needs to know that the applicant has the capacity to know what went wrong or what could be improved on. Self-awareness and openness to learning and personal change are useful traits in distinguishing between an average and a superior candidate. The interviewer can test for these traits by asking the following questions:

- Have you changed how you do things since your experience with that project?
- If you were to do a similar assignment again what would you do differently to get an even better result?
- How have your skills improved over time?
- What can you do more quickly, with fewer errors and higher quality?

Avoid Taking Things at Face Value

In assessing the calibre of interviewees' answers, look at:

- What *impact* their decisions and actions had
- The level of *personal involvement* of the interviewee in bringing about the result
- The degree of *difficulty* of opposition that they had to overcome

Always be alert to the fact that you cannot take anything you hear at face value; instead, you must evaluate both the accuracy and the significance of what you are hearing.

What the pros say: ✓

- Competency-based interviewing is a particular method of interviewing candidates that gives a focussed, objective and fair way of assessing whether each candidate has the right level of attainment for each and every competency you want them to have. It is not the only structured form of interview, but it is the most common. It is in a state of constant evolution.
- Competency-based interviewing can become a straight-jacket for interviewers if it is used too rigidly; it is best used as part of a range of techniques that pull together to get the most complete picture.
- Look at the depth, range and complexity of the examples the candidate gives you and use this information to compare and contrast one candidate with another.
- Failure to produce satisfactory evidence of effective performance on any one of the key competencies is a deal-breaker and is enough to eliminate a candidate, no matter how good they are in other areas.
- Many interviewees offer generic answers which are not based on their own experience. Using the competency model gives you a method for drilling down into their actual experiences, exposing those who never had the experience in the first place.
- Use an acronym such as EARL to help you remember how to sequence your questions.

The lazy interviewer: ✕

- Takes any plausible example of competence and settles for a story which is well told
- Lets the well-prepared candidate take control by letting them tell their story without probing for details and proofs
- Doesn't challenge generalisations or inflated examples
- Doesn't deviate from the script, but doggedly asks the same questions of all candidates without allowing for the diversity of answers that each candidate will give
- Doesn't bother to get to the heart of the matter
- Isn't clear about the levels of performance required in the job – has a hazy notion of the competencies
- Allows the candidate to use 'we' statements without probing for their individual performance and contribution

The best interviewers: ✓

- Bunch competencies into four or five key groupings rather than have a long, unstructured wish list
- Are realistic enough to know that they can explore only a small number of competencies in depth – especially if they are using something like the EARL structure
- Are versatile in their choice of questions and cleverly intertwine the full range of probing techniques with the competency framework so as to get a useful and real exchange going
- Set the agenda for the interview by choosing what examples they want to delve into, rather than letting the interviewee play to their preferred agenda

- Recognise trite or simplistic examples of experience for what they are
- Can rate examples of competencies accurately and consistently across a number of interviews

---

Coaches' Corner – Things for You to Try

- Develop some model question sequences that you can use to probe any one area of expertise, e.g. problem solving, business development, sales skills and techniques.
- Consider how many different ways you might ask, 'Can you give me an example of …?'
- Consider how the competencies required to do certain jobs might evolve due to changing market conditions of technologies.

8

Unravelling the Answers

Provoking Questions

- *X may well do a great interview, but will they perform brilliantly or be a disappointment in the job, and how can you spot that during the interview?*
- *Can the interviewees' answers reveal who the real performers are?*

In this chapter you will learn how to:

- Unravel the answers
- Assess the information offered
- Spot the star performers
- Eliminate the duds
- Deal with misrepresentation
- Spot the coached candidate

Real-life Experience

It had been a long series of interviews – over 20 in all – and Hilary felt that most of the candidates presented very well, but she couldn't help getting the feeling that some were misrepresenting themselves; some may even have been lying in their desperation to get the job. Her dilemma was how to test the candidates' skills and experience properly, but without the interview becoming confrontational.

It is not good enough just to get the interviewee talking – they have to deliver the evidence that they know what the job entails, that they have done something like it before and that they will be able to deliver in the future.

When it comes to hiring, the general thinking seems to be that once a candidate or interviewee performs well at interview, they will perform well on the job. But what constitutes a good interviewee? Obviously, the right information will let you decide whether the interviewee is simply well practised at interviewing or a performer who can deliver on the job. It is up to you as the interviewer to be critical in assessing the answers you get in response to your questions.

Dealing with Misrepresentation: Can You Believe All the Interviewee Tells You?

It can be easier than you think to be taken in by an interviewee who 'talks the good talk'. To be fair, interviewees are programmed to project themselves in the best possible light and, either intentionally or unintentionally, they will put a certain gloss on events and experiences. We all tend to do this when we sit in the interviewee chair, and we do it because we do not want to let ourselves down.

Sometimes by asking questions that are too general we give a platform to the interviewee to make sweeping statements, such as, 'I'm a firm believer in the power of positive thinking,' or, 'I always lead from the front.'

Unravelling the Answers: What Am I Getting Here?

What you are looking for is hard evidence of past performance and a clear match between the interviewee's knowledge, skills and experience and the job you are looking to fill. Be alert if it sounds like the interviewee is in storytelling mode and they are taking too much time to answer your questions. Be prepared to interrupt early to divert a long and boring answer; this can be done tactfully, and it helps the interviewee as well by focussing their answer.

In Chapter 7 we looked at the EARL structure, a competency-based framework of questions which allows the interviewer to assess the interviewee's level of experience and achievement in a structured way by seeking examples of Experience, Actions taken, Results achieved and Learning gained. However, as the following chart indicates, in order to use your time during the interview effectively you will need to focus mainly on the action stage, which will give you evidence of skills, expertise and achievement:

EARL: Interview Time Allocation

Stage	Purpose	Time Allocated
Experience	To establish the breadth and depth of experience and to select an appropriate example to probe in further detail	No more than 10%
Actions	To get a description of what the interviewee did, why they did it, what they were trying to achieve, what options they explored, etc.	60%
Results	To establish what results were achieved using relevant metrics (e.g. sales, saving and yield) to record as proofs of performance	20%
Learning	To establish what lessons were learned and have been applied	10%

Once you get the structure into your head you can be much more focussed on unravelling the candidate's answers. The candidate may try and divert you by going into side issues, but it is your job to re-direct them, as follows:

Interviewee: 'We made the campaign a model for others to follow; we were featured on the business show on Radio 1 …'

Interviewer: 'I would be more interested in looking at your particular contribution.'

Diversionary Tactics

A weak interviewee may exaggerate their performance in a number of ways. The table overleaf shows you how to deal with some of the more common diversionary tactics used by interviewees.

Getting Past the Smokescreen

Weak interviewees who know they are short on hard facts, results and achievements will try every trick in the book to fill the space with plausible-sounding guff. Think of yourself as an investigative journalist who needs salient facts when interviewing a politician so as to complete an investigative piece. Some politicians may bluster, speculate and divert, but the journalist has the other pieces of the jigsaw and knows exactly what they are looking for to complete the story. Think of yourself as that journalist: you have the CV and other evidence, but there are some bits of the jigsaw missing; you have to be sure that you have all the pieces and that they fit together properly.

Tackling Diversionary Tactics

Tactic	Your Strategy	Your Response
1. Irrelevant background information: 'We were the market leader for three years running.'	Focus on your objective	'What I am looking for is how your sales improved.'
2. Generalisations: 'Well-briefed staff always perform well.'	Challenge woolly thinking	'Can you think of a situation where a well-briefed team failed to deliver?'
3. Strong belief statements: 'I have always firmly believed in the company's values.'	Translate belief into action	'How has that value system affected the way you work?'
4. Feelings: 'I feel we got a good result.'	Feelings are not facts	'How did you measure your success?'
5. Speculation: 'Social media are the only future for marketing.'	Uncover depth of thinking	'What other options have you considered?'

Seven Strategies to Sharpen Your Investigative Skills

While you do not want to start out interviewing on the assumption that you can believe none of what you hear, you will need to sharpen your skills of detection to make sure you are getting the truth, using some of the strategies outlined below.

Strategy 1: Find and Explore Gaps

The story you are being told may not be complete. Ask yourself what is missing. If one point is being emphasised, what is it drawing you away from? For instance, if someone is trying to sell you their car at a good price you might ask yourself, why such a good price? Is it a stolen car? Was it in a crash? When the interviewee comes back again and again to a particular job or experience rather than another, why is this? Is it because they didn't perform so well in some of their other jobs or is it because they genuinely shone best in that particular job because the job allowed them to?

Strategy 2: Test Chains of Logical Statements

Candidates use logic chains to persuade: be prepared to test the links. For example:

> **Interviewer:** 'Do you have the right level of analytical skills for this work?'
> **Interviewee:** I have an MSc in the subject ...'
> **Interviewer:** 'In what way has that helped you in your previous job?'

Interviewee: 'The Masters was research based, so it wouldn't have been directly relevant to my work; I know a lot about the subject though.'

In this case the interviewee has failed to convince the interviewer that their expertise would apply directly to the vacancy.

Strategy 3: Make Sure Statements Have the Right Weight

Use probing questions to make sure you are giving the right weight to what you hear, as follows:

Interviewee: 'I dealt with the whole area of customer complaints.'
Interviewer: 'And exactly what did that involve?'
Interviewee: 'I logged the complaints so we had a record of all the details, including dates and names.'

When the interviewer probes for further detail it is apparent that the interviewee's level of responsibility is low and, worse than that, their concept of what it means to 'handle' complaints is worryingly narrow and lacks any sense of the importance of proactivity.

Strategy 4: Ignore Irrelevancies

Interviewees will often give a lot of detail about the company they have worked for, the product or service they provided, particular technologies their current company uses, etc. You may need to hear some of this to get some context, but don't allow the candidate to get sidetracked into talking about 'it' or 'them'.

Strategy 5: Differentiate Between Opinions and Behaviour

Just because someone expresses an opinion about something doesn't mean they live by that view in practice. For example:

> **Interviewee:** 'I think all good managers should give their staff the opportunity to make suggestions for change/improvement.'

To investigate this statement further, the interviewer needs to respond with the following type of question:

> **Interviewer:** 'Can you give me an example of when you have done this and how you went about it? And with what success?'

Strategy 6: Differentiate Between Low- and High-level Examples

A frequent problem is that interviewees give examples of achievements that are at an inferior level to what you need in the job you are recruiting for. While the example they give might sound relevant, by probing for detail you can get a sense of the level of their skill, as illustrated in the examples below.

> ## Low-level Example
>
> **Interviewer:** 'Can you give me an example of when you led a team?'
> **Interviewee:** 'I was the head of the social committee in work for three years running.'
> **Interviewer:** 'What did that involve?'
> **Interviewee:** 'We had to organise the Christmas party each year and we collected money for a nominated charity ...'

What the above example tells you is that the interviewee has a narrow experience of managing an informal group, which didn't have a very demanding remit. In the example they chose to give the interviewer they have given no strong evidence that they had an opportunity to show a range of leadership skills.

By contrast, the following example given by another interviewee has enough scope to show that they took actions that resulted in a successful and significant outcome:

> ## High-level Example
>
> Here the EARL framework has been used to show how the candidate demonstrates their experience (E), actions (A), results (R) and learning (L):
> **Interviewer:** 'Can you give me an example of when you led a team?'
> **Interviewee:** 'I was recruited from a rival company because I had ten years' experience of leading

high performance teams (E). It was the first time team-working had been tried. I had led teams before (E), but this was really difficult: I had no clear instruction from above, apart from the delivery date, sales targets and budget available. I had no instructions on how to set up the team and, initially, I had no support from the eight members of the team. Over a six-month period I managed to get increasing levels of buy-in by *delegating key tasks* (A). I became really involved in *challenging and changing* (A) a way of thinking that had dominated the place for twenty years. I tried a number of strategies – not all of them successful or right in the situation. I won over the team one-by-one (R), but in the end I *achieved the targets* set for us [*gives details*] (R), and I got the team pulling together in a way that they had never experienced before. I *learned how to deal with feedback, challenge poor results and how to raise performance levels* (L). The team now runs itself. Since then, I have been asked to lead a few start-up teams in other areas.

Strategy 7: Get the Context When the Interviewee Quotes Facts

When the interviewee quotes facts, figures or results you need to get background information to put them into perspective, i.e. what are the standards and what are the norms? For example:

Interviewer: 'How good a sales executive were you?'
Interviewee: 'I brought in over two hundred thousand Euros worth of business last year.'

What you might not be told – unless you ask – is that the two hundred thousand was small fry for a company of that size with a high value, niche product. Similarly, be wary when interviewees quote percentages or other figures, as follows:

Interviewer: 'How good a sales executive were you?'
Interviewee: 'I sold 50 per cent more than the previous job holder had the year before.'

In a situation such as this, it is important to find out what the base line in figures is for the comparison, i.e. what the actual sales target was. Get the information in its correct context. What you might not hear is that the previous incumbent was fired for poor performance! Ask yourself, 'What am I getting here? Performance at a more junior level than I am really looking for?'

Spot the Star Performers

To spot a star performer, look out for those who:

- Take their time to listen to the question carefully and answer the question thoughtfully
- Let you finish your question and actually answer the question you asked
- Show that they understand the job specification and help you match the depth and breadth of their experience to the demands of the job

- Provide hard evidence of what they have done in terms that are relevant to the job they are applying for
- Give specific examples to illustrate their skills and experience
- Show that they have learned from past experiences by giving evidence of how they have applied their learning in action
- Can be concise or expansive on demand
- Correct your question with the right answer (e.g. if you asked a closed question, but you actually needed more information than the question suggested)

Weak interviewees are conspicuous in their answers by the absence of the above!

Eliminate the Duds

Poor interviewees reveal themselves by:

- Not listening to the question
- Rushing into their answers
- Giving generic 'one-size-fits-all' answers
- Being unaware of what the job is about
- Using a lot of 'we' statements
- Talking in generalities
- Speaking a lot about 'what I would do if …'
- Answering a completely different question to the one that was asked
- Being so reticent with their answers that they are 'hard work' for the interviewer

Extreme Situations: Waffling or Lying

While in normal social interaction it may seem rude to interrupt when someone is speaking, different rules apply in a job interview. The tendency to be polite makes many interviewers reluctant to interrupt, even when the interviewee is waffling or possibly lying, but you will need to move beyond the rapport-building techniques outlined in Chapter 5 to deal with the two extreme situations discussed below.

Situation 1: Redirecting the Waffling Interviewee

When an interviewee is waffling on and appears to be unstoppable, you will need a range of escalated responses to redirect their speech. If the interviewee hasn't given a clear answer within about 30 seconds of starting their response, be prepared to intervene. Summarise what you have heard and tell the interviewee that you need a concise answer to your question. If that doesn't work you may have to be more assertive. Remind the candidate that time is critical and be directive in what you are looking for. You should be polite but also assertive in your interruption. It is best to operate a graduated approach, as follows:

Begin gently: 'Thank you; sorry to interrupt, but I need you to focus on the following element …'

Steer towards what you want to cover: 'What you are telling me is … What I would like you to focus on is …' This is useful because it shows the interviewee that you are listening actively and with understanding to what they are saying.

Resort to a pointed remark: this should be used *only* if the interviewee seems to be ignoring subtle hints to be more concise. You must be direct: 'I know I have interrupted you already, but to help me get the best view of your abilities I need clear evidence on how you guided your team.'

Before you write the candidate off, be sure that you have explored all avenues to get the information you need.

Situation 2: You Suspect the Interviewee May Be Lying

Given the high figures of people who misrepresent facts on their CVs, the interviewer may need to be skilled in detecting where there has been misrepresentation in the interviewee's answer. The job is made much more difficult by the fact that interviewees can be untruthful with statements that are mostly true and are very plausible; they may also withhold information that they think will show them in a bad light.

If you are not sure you are getting the truth, probe, probe, probe, summarise and probe some more. As you do, tune into the interviewee's body language. Do they appear under stress? Are their answers consistent? Is their tone of voice and eye contact relatively consistent or are there sudden changes in the way they are presenting themselves? Does their eye contact shift away from you as they are telling you something? Do they start to move around in their chair?

If you suspect that an interviewee may be exaggerating or lying, there are a number of options open to you. We do not recommend the direct approach to challenge deliberate misrepresentation: it is unacceptable and unprofessional behaviour to accuse an interviewee of lying. The following subtle approaches may be more fruitful:

The power of summary: 'Can I summarise what you are saying to me ... Have I got this right?'

Use a well chosen question to check inconsistencies: the effect can be in inverse proportion to the gentleness of the question: 'Can you then tell me how you were doing that in Paris when your CV says you were full-time on a different assignment in Dublin?'

A subtle warning: 'Some people would have difficulty with that statement. How would you convince them?'

Scarcity value: 'That is an interesting, though rare, take on the situation. It doesn't seem to reflect what usually happens. How would you justify this exception to the rule?'

No going back: 'I am not sure that your details stack up because of the gaps in the answers you have given already. Would you like to reconsider what you have said to me so far?'

Magic tricks work because the magician gets you to focus on one thing so as to draw you away from something they do not want you to see. Things as presented may only be part of the story and, just like a good journalist, you need to get the full story.

Spotting the Coached Candidate

Many interviewers find themselves dealing with candidates who have put far more time into preparing for the interview than the interviewers themselves and who have learned to practice the dark art of 'spin'. Sometimes the level of coaching the candidate has received is obvious from their demeanour and polished answers. At other times, however, this is not so easy to spot.

Some Warning Signs

Beware of the interviewee who:

- Never admits to making a mistake
- Presents failures as learning opportunities – without showing how the learning is applied
- When asked about weaknesses, usually picks one that is a spin on a strength, such as, 'My main weakness is that I get a bit impatient with people who arrive late for meetings,' thus implying that they are a very good timekeeper!
- Seldom takes time to reflect before answering a searching question
- Is short on detail and facts, especially about their work history
- Appears confident and fluid, but their answers are almost too perfect, as if they have been learned off
- When asked a difficult question that they can't answer answers a slightly different question instead
- Rattles off information about your company in an encyclopaedic fashion

- Tries to play the role of the 'perfect' candidate who has never put a foot wrong and shows no insightfulness into their character
- Uses generic descriptions of themselves with lots of jargon words
- When asked at the end of the interview if they have any questions, jumps in to give a sales pitch as to why you should hire them

Strategies for Interviewing Coached Candidates

Increasingly, candidates are paying consultants to help them improve their level of performance at interview; you will need to be alert to the fruits of their efforts! The following are some useful strategies:

Explore breadth and depth of experience: instead of looking for one example of a competency, explore such things as years of experience and typical versus untypical situations.

Focus on specific time and place: this will ensure the examples you are given are particular rather than generalisations.

Probe answers: do not let the candidate dominate the conversation.

Don't be afraid to interrupt: if it seems like you are getting a very polished answer, interrupt the interviewee – observe whether they are as fluent following the interruption.

Observe non-verbal behaviour: changes in tone of voice, inflexion or eye contact may indicate a change from a rehearsed segment. Watch for signs of the interviewee guiding you towards one theme – and away from another. Probe the other!

Challenge the interviewee's answer: in extreme situations you may have to challenge the interviewee's answer: 'That sounds very neat, but could you give me an example of another situation where things didn't run too smoothly?'

What the pros say: ✓

- Weak interviewees start answering the question they think you are asking while you are still asking it!
- A worryingly high proportion of interviewees will lie or misrepresent information.
- Weak interviewees haven't researched the job or the industry in depth.
- Weak interviewees may have been coached to be fluent in their answers to hide their lack of depth and breadth of experience.
- Well coached, weak interviewees may score better than they deserve to because of their fluent answers.
- Many interviewees are better trained than their interviewers.

The lazy interviewer: ✗

- Sits back once the interviewee is in full flight
- Takes information at face value
- Doesn't explore context

- Waits for information that confirms their preconceptions
- Assumes that a talkative interviewee who sells their track record is the best person for the job

The best interviewers: ✓

- Listen to the answers critically and are aware of the structure of the answer
- Have a clear idea of the range of answers they may get
- Have a clear understanding of what they're looking for, the levels of performance expected, results achieved, essential and desirable skills and expertise, etc.
- Are open to different interpretations of information – rather than taking it at face value
- Have a wide range of communication skills and can deal with all interviewees from the shyest to the most verbose
- Focus on what's relevant
- Can distinguish the good talker from the good candidate

Coaches' Corner – Things for You to Try

- Scan some of the material available to jobseekers on how to be interviewed well and how to sell yourself at interview. See if you can spot these techniques at the next interview you conduct.
- Observe colleagues who chair meetings well to get through the agenda.
- Practice mannerly interruptions in your business meetings and in discussions with colleagues to develop your skills of polite interruption.

9

Keeping It Legal

Provoking Questions

- *Have you any idea what biases we have lurking below the surface that get in the way of making sound decisions about who we should hire and who we should not hire?*
- *Do you know how easy it is for a disappointed applicant to raise a legal challenge about how they were treated before or during an interview?*
- *Can you imagine the time commitment and stress involved if you have to deal with a case taken against you?*

In this chapter you will learn:

- How to be more aware of the effects of bias
- How to focus on being fair
- Your legal obligations
- The most common types of legal challenges
- How best to interview a candidate with a disability
- How to stay out of legal hot water with job ads

Real-life Experience

Joanne worked for a busy company that wanted to hire someone urgently to replace an employee who had walked out, without giving any notice, at the busiest time of the year for the company. The company had a preference for people who were outgoing, positive and young in their approach. They would want her to find somebody who could fit easily and quickly into the company culture without the need for any adjustments or special treatment. She wondered if this would present any problems during the interview process.

Wired To Be Biased

Our background, upbringing, education and life experiences all influence our thinking about other people. We are quick to make judgements about others, either positive or negative. Much of the time we are not aware of what biases affect our judgements; even those who feel they are very open to people of different backgrounds will be full of preconceptions. When it comes to selecting new hires these preconceptions will influence our views and sometimes get in the way of seeing who the best candidate really is. In extreme cases, our biases may spill over into a level of racism, discrimination, unfair or possibly illegal treatment of applicants.

Interviewers can be biased in either a direct or indirect way. The more blatant form of bias is more easily recognisable: sometimes employers have an aversion to people of a particular age group, nationality, gender, family status, etc. As awareness of the need for equal opportunities for all people is increasing, many employers now know what fair employment practices are, although a trawl through the numerous cases taken against employers by disgruntled job applicants every year would tell you there are still many unscrupulous employers out there who discriminate strongly against certain people or groups! There are also many who inadvertently get on the wrong side of the law. This chapter will help you to stay out of trouble and will give you the tools to apply fairness to your selection process so as to get the best out of candidates.

Saints and Devils

For many people, the risk of prejudice lies in an indirect form of bias, often something that we are unaware of. We make all kinds of assumptions about people based on tiny snippets of information about them. These assumptions may be either positive or negative. Ignorance and cultural stereotypes may blind us to the strengths of some potential candidates.

One of the most common flaws of interviewers is that they generalise either positively or negatively based on one fact alone – what are generally referred to as the *halo* and *horn* effects.

These generalisations spring from overvaluing certain traits or from assuming that because someone shines in one area they must also be good in other areas (the halo effect). The opposite of this can also happen where the interviewer's negative evaluation of one aspect of the candidate's characteristics spills over into a generalised negative feeling about their complete application (the horn effect). In either case, we selectively filter information to support our initial (positive or negative) judgement. To illustrate what we mean, look at the following example showing how a piece of information from a job applicant can be interpreted in different ways by interviewers:

The Halo and Horn Effects in Practice

The person being interviewed has been travelling abroad for the past two years, picking up a range of jobs, many of which are not directly related to the job they are now applying for.

Response of Interviewer 1

This person has proved to be self-sufficient, flexible and willing to take risks. They have had to deal with lots of different people and situations; they will therefore find it easy to get on well with colleagues and customers here. They now have the wanderlust out of their system, so they will be likely to want to stay with us for some time.

Response of Interviewer 2

This person gave up a perfectly good job to go walkabout for nearly two years; that shows a tendency to act impulsively and be self-centred. None of the work they did while travelling is relevant, and they may take a long time to settle down after being away for so long. They haven't had to stick at the same thing for longer than they cared to, so they may get bored and restless easily.

In the above example we have the same objective fact, but it is viewed very differently by the two interviewers. As interviewers, we tend to rush to judgement mode. Instead, what we need to do is put each piece of information into context: get enough background information to know for certain that we are moving towards the correct conclusion. After an interview be prepared to argue the toss with other interviewers if you differ in your interpretation of the facts. Always ask yourself, 'What exactly did I pick up from the interviewee to draw me to this conclusion?'

We have come across countless similar examples of interviewers jumping to conclusions based on aspects of a candidate's background, such as the following:

The hobbies they are interested in: the interviewer assumes that the candidate who plays a minority sport is strange, idiosyncratic and wouldn't 'fit in'.

The school they went to: the interviewer assumes all graduates from a well-known private school have the qualities for which the school is noteworthy.

The qualification they possess: if a job applicant has a PhD in a highly technical specialty, for example, the interviewer interprets this one fact to mean that they might be a geek, aloof or maybe a poor team player rather than looking through all the information to get a more balanced, accurate view.

The company they worked for: the interviewer assumes the candidate is innovative and technically brilliant because they worked for a rapidly expanding, high-tech competitor company.

The job they currently have: the interviewer assumes the candidate who is working as a team leader in a service delivery role has all the strengths of a good team leader.

How Biased Are *You*?

Apart from aspects of the candidate's background and work experience that seem to launch us into flawed judgements, there are also elements of the candidate's appearance, demeanour and behaviour at interview that will have those bias juices running within seconds of the interview starting. To get a sense of what biases *you* might have lurking below the surface, see what your responses are to the following situations:

Situation 1: Intense or Organised?

You meet a tall, thin, neatly-dressed young woman, Maria, who speaks and moves quickly. Do you assume she is a bit intense and prone to nervousness (that might result in an inability to handle stress and pressure well) or do you view her as someone who looks organised, methodical and will get things done quickly?

Situation 2: Nervous or Keen?

Ian arrives for interview looking sweaty and nervous. Do you assume this person will be unsuitable because, if they can't handle the stress at interview, they will be unable to handle the stress of the job, or do you view the candidate as someone who is really keen to get this job?

Situation 3: Nonconformist or Difficult?

Neil presents for interview as a brilliant financial analyst and a bit of a maverick. He says he doesn't play the corporate game. After all, why dress up when you are not going to be meeting clients face to face? You may value his disinclination to conform as an indication that he will provide a useful alternative view when key decisions are being taken within your management team, or you may take his dress code as a signal that he may be difficult to manage.

Interpreting How a Candidate Dresses for Interview

Anecdotal evidence suggests to us that we have problems with lots of aspects of people's appearance, behaviour and record when we come to interview them and, more recently as a society, we seem to place greater emphasis on appearance than ever before. However, it is legitimate as an interviewer to assess whether a candidate indicates through their dress that they understand the company's culture and have also been sufficiently motivated to take the trouble to dress appropriately. Bear in mind that what constitutes appropriate dress in one context might be wholly inappropriate in another.

A pleasant appearance is rated highly, but what about all those who are too thin, too fat, balding, wear glasses, dress unflatteringly, have a high-pitched voice, have an accent, talk slowly, talk fast ... The list is endless and leaves us wondering if any of us has a chance of being viewed objectively and fairly! We sometimes too readily write off those who are a little different.

Legal Obligations

As an interviewer of job applicants you are bound by certain laws. The laws that most directly affect you are the Employment Equality Acts 1998 and 2004. These Acts state that you may not discriminate either directly or indirectly against an applicant for a job or for promotion on any of nine prohibited grounds. When they talk of discrimination they mean treating a person or a group less favourably than another group. The nine prohibited grounds are as follows:

1. Gender
2. Civil status
3. Family status
4. Sexual orientation
5. Religious belief
6. Age
7. Disability
8. Race, colour, nationality, ethnic or national origins
9. Membership of the Traveller community

You are also forbidden by law to write anything discriminatory in a job advertisement.

Some Nasty Surprises

Most of the cases taken by dissatisfied candidates for employment and for promotion at work are dealt with by the Equality Tribunal. The Equality Officers attached to the Tribunal have the power to enter premises and to see all documentation relating to the filling of a vacancy, either for a new hire or for internal promotion purposes. You need to remember this when you're scribbling a few notes in the margin of an applicant's CV, as you might be rightly embarrassed if all your scribbles and hieroglyphics are demanded by the Equality Officer to assist them in examining the rights and wrongs of a case some months later! They have the legal power to ask you to give evidence, and by that time you might not be able to remember exactly what you asked during the interview and why exactly you rated the candidate in the way you did.

Even when you believe you are in the right and have been very thorough in your shortlisting, interviewing and final selection, you might be quite surprised to find that through one unintentional word or action you give a disappointed candidate a vehicle for taking and winning a case against you.

The law places the burden on the employer to prove that no discrimination has taken place, once facts are established from which it can be presumed that there is a case to be answered.

Examples of what may be considered discriminatory or inappropriate behaviour include the following:

- Having only one person do the shortlisting of candidates
- Not keeping notes from the screening stage
- Not having written criteria for shortlisting
- Insisting on a particular qualification that was not available before a recent date, which might be construed as discrimination on age grounds

- Asking a candidate questions about their background as part of the polite chat in bringing the candidate from the reception area to the interview room
- Asking an interviewee why they would want the hassle of a more senior job at 'this stage of their life'
- Writing 'wears a hearing aid' in the margins of the application form, or similarly taking note of an obvious disability
- Not keeping written records of the interviewers' scoring of candidates
- Interviewers not ranking candidates separately and independently before coming to a consensus decision
- Lacking transparency in consensus marking
- Giving the results of an interview over the phone rather than in writing
- Not facilitating a deaf candidate by allowing enough time to arrange for a sign language expert to accompany him or her to the interview
- Contacting referees before the interview regarding matters unrelated to the references; for instance, asking a previous employer about aspects of the candidate's experience that are not being sought in your marking scheme
- Failing to keep records of the interview processes, which in and of itself may not be discriminatory, but when coupled with other factors may lead a court to infer that there has been discrimination

Keeping Yourself Honest

It is important that you do not come to a conclusion about a candidate and then try to fit your documenting of the interview to suit your conclusion. If you do so you run the risk that your own personal biases become the controlling factor in your hiring decision, rather than the genuine suitability of the candidate. An Equality Officer will easily see that you have 'cooked the books'. As one Officer who was investigating a case taken against an employer noted:

> The only conclusion I can reach from this examination is that the interview board arrived at an overall impression as to the relative suitability of the candidates and then afterwards set about allocating or adjusting marks under the six headings [or criteria]. The marks appear to have been allocated to candidates within certain ranges in order to give each candidate an overall placing consistent with the overall impression.

Employers have also been found, on occasion, to have been too general in what they wrote about candidates who did not get an offer of employment. When one candidate in such a situation took a case for discrimination, the employer was on weak ground because they had written the same reason of unsuitability for all unsuccessful candidates: they were all lacking the 'necessary management and leadership skills for the post'.

A further example of discrimination which was hidden within the interview marking scheme was uncovered in a case where the Equality Officer concluded that candidates were discriminated against on the basis of their age. The Officer stated:

Their ages had become a factor in how the interview board viewed their suitability for the posts,
and the interview board awarded them inexplicably
low marks under every criterion on which they
were marked.

Candidates with a Disability

The law expects you to make reasonable effort to accommo-
date a candidate with a disability so they can attend for
interview. It also expects you to make reasonable effort to
provide a suitable working environment for a disabled candidate who is successful at interview. The Equality Tribunal
does not expect you to have to spend the company's profits
making changes to facilitate someone with a disability, but it
will expect you to absorb modest costs in order to facilitate a
worker with a disability. Your lack of suitable facilities, such
as a ramp for a wheelchair, will not be seen as a reasonable
excuse for not hiring a disabled person who is suitable for the
job in all other respects.

Health problems such as chronic back problems, asthma,
alcoholism, dyslexia and migraine are just some of the
conditions that may be viewed as forms of disability. When
you seek a medical reference from a candidate you need to
be careful how you assess the opinion of the medical referee.
If the referee indicates that the candidate may at some future
time be more susceptible to the disability or health problem
but is currently fit for work you should seek a medical reference from a specialist, and only where the specialist states
definitively that the health issue will seriously impinge on a

person's capacity to perform the job will you be free to reject the candidate.

You must be alert to the possibility that a person with a disability may suffer discrimination not because of their disability, but because they are perceived to be less capable or less dependable than a person without a disability.

Keeping Your Advertisements Free From Discrimination

When you advertise a vacancy, avoid using phrases such as the following:

- Young and dynamic
- A maximum of two to three years commercial experience
- School-leaver
- More than ten years' experience, if that amount of experience is not absolutely relevant
- Specific experience in this country or knowledge of the local context, unless absolutely essential to the job
- Mature lady required
- Local person preferred
- Valid work permit required
- Committed person with no ties

What the pros say: ✓

- Ask yourself if all candidates had a comparable interview experience and were treated similarly.
- Only ask questions that you can stand over because they are rooted in the requirements of the job.

- Put your hunches, social stereotypes and pet psychological theories aside when you go to interview applicants.
- Don't get fussed about your legal obligations as an interviewer: think in terms of applying best interview practice to get the most suitable person and, indirectly, you will also be keeping yourself out of legal hot water.

The lazy interviewer: ✗

- Relies on their 'gut feeling' about candidates without taking the time to assess each person objectively
- Allows their personal prejudices to get in the way of making a good hire
- Neglects to keep proper interview records and detailed marking schemes for each candidate

The best interviewers: ✓

Are prepared before, during and after the interview.

Before the interview they:

- Don't specifically ask for a date of birth on a job application form
- Decide on what the criteria are for both shortlisting and selection before they go through the applications
- Base the criteria on the detail of the job and person spec
- Make sure those criteria are relevant, objective, clear and written down

During the interview they:

- Have more than one interviewer making the selection
- Have gender balance among the selectors
- Treat all candidates similarly: probe the same areas with each person
- Don't ask for information that is not directly relevant to the job
- Never ask questions about someone's marital or family status, how many children they have, who minds the children, what their partner works at, etc.
- Never comment on what someone is wearing or how they look
- Provide assistance to candidates with a disability to make it possible for them to attend and to have a comfortable interview environment
- Don't ask someone with an obvious disability how they will manage to do the job; if physical ability is relevant to the job, a medical examination should be used to determine the suitability of final candidates.

After the interview they:

- Mark each candidate straight away and make notes about the interview
- Each mark separately before conferring with other interviewers
- Make sure they link their assessment directly to the criteria they have already decided on

- Use very specific reasons for excluding a candidate and avoid using criteria such as 'general suitability'
- Only record what has been said in the interview and how the selection decision was made, not their beliefs or thoughts about the candidate, i.e. they note *facts* rather than impressions
- Keep written records of the marking scheme and how decisions on marking were arrived at
- Keep a clear record of the objective criteria applied in deciding not to call applicants for interview
- Hold records for one year after the interview takes place

Coaches' Corner – Things for You to Try

- Have a look at the website for the Equality Tribunal (www. equalitytribunal.ie) to read about some of the cases that have been taken against employers for discrimination so you can get a sense of what can go wrong for interviewers.
- Engage in discussion with colleagues and friends on the topic of bias and pet hates – you'll be amazed at where those discussions might lead you, and they will help you become more aware of the whole subject of bias.

Health Warning

You may think that what we are advising in this chapter is over the top, but our advice is based on the case law that has developed over many years. The best way to keep on the right side of the law is to have a rigorous set of selection procedures and practices, based on a soundly thought-out view of what exactly you want from the ideal candidate and a thorough scrutiny of your candidates based on that view. Apart from any legal obligations, that is what you need to do to make sure you're getting the right person for the job, so do not write off this chapter as 'political correctness' gone mad.

10

Making the Final Decision

Provoking Question

- *When the interviewing is over, how will you use all you have heard during the interviews to decide who should be offered the job?*

In this chapter you will learn how to:

- Draw up an appropriate marking scheme
- Understand what pitfalls can occur in rating candidates
- Get the best from references

Real-life Experience

Rachel and Alan had interviewed fifteen candidates for two vacancies. They also had the results of aptitude tests and technical presentations to hand. They had been thorough at interview, spending an hour with each candidate, along with preliminary interviews and aptitude testing, so they had lots of information to hand. There were two obviously unsuitable candidates, and quite a number that didn't match up fully, but was there an obvious first and second choice at the top end? Despite all their time and effort so far, it seemed the hardest part of the selection process still lay ahead.

Marking Schemes

In Chapter 2 we looked at drawing up a marking scheme for shortlisting purposes that was directly linked to the job and could be used to choose who to call for interview. A more comprehensive version than this is needed for marking candidates, based on the selection criteria you have chosen and upon which you have based your interview. The marking scheme is used for comparing candidates to each other and for helping you decide who the most suitable person from the group is. It can be integrated into the interview notes if you prefer to have only one document. The marking scheme should have the following elements:

- A shortlist of relevant criteria that in total tells the full story of what the ideal candidate should have in terms of experience, expertise and personal qualities
- No overlap between the criteria
- A weighting or priority assigned to any criterion that you think is more important than the others
- A decision on whether there is a minimum mark that must be reached on any or all of the criteria, and below which a candidate will be discounted, no matter what

their total score is. For instance, you may feel that lack of the appropriate level of technical knowhow is a dealbreaker, even though the candidate has all the other qualities you want in abundance.

- Scope to document what 'evidence' you heard from the candidate that you used as the basis for your scoring (see example below)
- Inclusion of ratings from other selection aids, such as group exercises, presentations, etc., if you have not already taken them into account

Using the example of the customer care team leader from Chapter 2, a typical marking scheme for a large recruitment campaign might look like that in the table overleaf. Note that sample marking has been included in the table, and the total potential scores have been given in italics for each section.

Following completion of the marking scheme at interview stage, interviewers should include results from any other selection exercises used during the recruitment process, including any special comments relating to each candidate. Special comments should include points of concern and extra relevant information not allowed for in the marking scheme, such as reservations about whether the candidate will accept the job if offered it, practicality of commuting distance, whether there's enough scope in the job for the calibre of the individual, extra skills that would be useful to the company but not needed in the job, etc. Each interviewer should then record their total individual marks, as well as the total consensus marks amongst all interviewers, for each candidate.

Marking Scheme for a Customer Care Team Leader

Factor	Evidence	Score	Weighting	Weighted Score
Relevant Experience in Customer Care	Managed teams in three customer care roles	10	×3	Out of 30
	Customer high on her agenda Dealt well with complex issues in last job	8	×3	24
Leadership Ability	Set clear goals for staff Made clear what she wanted Coached weaker staff	10	×3	Out of 30 (min 20 needed)
	Delegated well under pressure before end-year results	7	×3	21
Interpersonal Skills	Could see things from staff point of view when motivation was poor	10	×2	Out of 20
	Dealt with conflict (boss) successfully	8	×2	16

(Continued)

Marking Scheme for a Customer Care Team Leader: (Continued)

Factor	Evidence	Score	Weighting	Weighted Score
Personal Organisation and Effectiveness	Met deadline when crisis demanded Cut backlog when asked to step in at short notice Very task-oriented	*10* 9	*None (×1)* x1	*Out of 10* 9
Analytical and Problem-solving Skills	Could dissect the problem of backlog into manageable parts Gave logical summary of what she would do in the first three months of the job	*10* 8	*None (×1)* x1	*Out of 10* 8
		Total		78/100

Simple Marking Schemes

The Simplest Marking System: –1, 0, +1

Under each major heading or competency the candidate is marked as follows:

- **–1** The candidate failed to provide evidence of the required level of competency.
- **0** The candidate provided satisfactory evidence of the required level of competency.
- **+1** The candidate provided evidence of higher than average levels of competency.

The beauty of this system is that if a candidate scores one –1 point, they are eliminated from further interviews. This marking system works well for an initial or preliminary set of interviews.

The Five-point Scale

This is similar to the five-point scale (1 to 5, with 1 being low and 5 being high) used in performance evaluation systems. The levels of suitability are rated as follows:

- **5** The candidate demonstrated exceptional levels of competence – typically less than 5 per cent of candidates will achieve this score.
- **4** The candidate demonstrated above-average levels of competence – typically approximately 10 per cent of candidates will achieve this score.

3 The candidate demonstrated adequate levels of competence with some minor gaps that can be dealt with by coaching or training on appointment.

2 The candidate demonstrated adequate levels of suitability in some competencies but lacked evidence in at least one major competency that could not be addressed by remedial coaching or training.

1 The candidate demonstrated little or no evidence of suitability in any of the competencies.

The main idea of this system is that a score of 1 or 2 in any of the major competencies will eliminate the candidate. There should be few scores of 4 and fewer scores of 5. This system is often used in competency-based interviewing.

Benchmarking

It is useful to get a sense of what is the basic entrance standard below which you would not accept a candidate, based on what you would consider to be adequate performance in the role you are interviewing for. If you are interviewing large numbers of candidates you will eventually find your benchmark within the group and you can then place all other candidates above or below this standard.

Pitfalls: What Can Go Wrong

Some of the more frequent errors in marking include:

• An inability to separate the middle ground

- Assigning marks to a generic heading like 'suitability', 'impression' or 'fit' that becomes the deciding factor when marking under other headings is very close
- Different interpretations of marks – easy and hard markers
- Loose job descriptions that increase the likelihood of individual interviewer's interpretations and bias
- Lack of clarity because of a lack of meaningful benchmarks

Marking Guidelines

- Each interviewer should mark individual candidates separately before conferring with other interviewers.
- Mark straight after each interview before you forget all the detail.
- Start with the assumption that the interviewee does not have the skill you are looking for and assign marks as the candidate reveals evidence of having the skill, i.e. start at zero and work up from there.
- Avoid the 'safe middle' when you're not sure what marks you should give; otherwise you will end up with a number of candidates with the same mark.
- Keep the normal distribution curve in mind: it is likely that there will be many geese, some ugly ducklings but only a few swans!
- Keep in mind earlier guidelines about bias.
- Be prepared to be convinced by the views of your fellow interviewers if they can support their views. At the same time, be prepared to be the one to convince your fellow

interviewers if you can support your view with factual details from the interview.
- Remember that no one person has the monopoly on insights.

Checking References

An accurate reference is the recruiter's best friend, but most of us have had the experience of being unable to get previous employers to provide the whole truth about a candidate for a variety of reasons. In some cases, the reference tells us more about the referee's motivations than it does about the candidate. For example, an unsatisfactory employee may be given a good reference to ease their exit from the company or as part of a deal if they are let go for reasons of poor performance. Equally, if the previous employer does not want to lose a good employee they may be less than enthusiastic in their praise in the hope that their lacklustre reference will discourage you from offering a job to this candidate. Most employers also prefer not to write anything too negative about someone out of feelings of loyalty or decency, or fear of a backlash. If an employee fails to get a job offer because of a negative reference from their current employer, the knowledge that a poor reference stymied their chances of moving on may leave them disgruntled and less motivated than before. Fear of legal action if an apparently unfavourable reference is given may also prevent an employer from telling you the whole truth about a candidate.

In order to get the best quality of information from a previous employer you need to channel appropriate questions that you would like them to answer rather than look for a general reference. You should give them a sense of the job you are hiring for so they can put their comments into that context. Your questions should seek to verify the following:

- The range and depth of experience that the candidate reported having
- The strengths and weaknesses they demonstrated in that role
- What value or contribution they made to the work of the company
- The candidate's level of flexibility and willingness to go the extra mile
- Sick leave and absence record – either specific or relative to the norm in the company
- The employer's view on whether they would be willing to consider rehiring this candidate at a future time
- Any aspects of the candidate's skills that would need training and mentoring (this is better than looking for a list of flaws that the employer may not want to divulge)
- Anything else of relevance that they think you should know

Code of Behaviour for Taking Up References

- If you can get the information you want via a phone call you may find you will get more honest information than you would from a written reference, and you can also pick up a certain amount from how things are said. Remember, sometimes what is not said is as telling as what is said.

- Always leave contacting a candidate's present employer until the last stage of the recruitment process and only contact them if you are in a position to make an offer subject to this reference being satisfactory.
- Ask the candidate's permission before checking with the current employer for a reference.
- Adhere to any promises of confidentiality that you have made to referees.
- Never rely on the open 'to whom it may concern' type of reference – it is too general to be of practical use.
- Get two or preferably more references. Never rely on just one reference.
- Don't be dictated to by the names of referees on the applicant's CV. They may be selective in who they put down as their referees.
- Seek out references from more recent employers rather than those from the distant past.
- Make sure you get information from the right source within the company: the line manager is usually best equipped to give you the most relevant detail. You can also consider getting references from co-workers, clients, customers, suppliers or others who have had regular and meaningful contact with the candidate.
- It may be policy in your company that the HR department looks after the taking up of references and making job offers.

Last-minute Reservations

There is a great feeling of accomplishment when you know you are about to make an offer to a candidate who is a clear winner and just what you were looking for or better! But it is not always so clear and straightforward.

The best advice we can give you in this book is this: *Do not make a job offer if you have any reservations!*

If you hear that little voice in your head expressing reservations, *listen* to it – it may save you a lot of hassle. It is possible that you did not get all the insights and information you wanted at the interview, despite your best efforts. In the final analysis you must err on the side of caution if at the last minute you are unsure.

Notwithstanding all we have advised regarding basing your decisions solidly on the facts you have elicited at the interview it is important to acknowledge and deal with any last-minute reservations that you have. It may be possible to meet with the final candidate once more to see if you can get some further certainty one way or the other. If at that point you continue to have reservations have the courage to decide not to make an offer. When you have spent a lot of time going through the interview process you will be reluctant to admit that you may have drawn a blank: all that work for nothing! However, most recruiters who have been in this position will tell you that when they had reservations at the final stage about a candidate but went on to select them anyway, they regretted that decision afterwards and paid a hefty price for it.

Before making a formal job offer, ask to see the preferred candidate once more. Perhaps ask a colleague to join you for this discussion. Talk through your reservations with the candidate; seek further feedback from referees and see whether this gives you more certainty one way or the other.

What the pros say: ✓

- Use a simple and relevant marking scheme to help you capture your assessment of each candidate.
- Your assessment of each candidate should be based firmly on the evidence of performance offered and what you heard them say during the interview.
- References are most useful when you ask the previous employer to answer specific questions about aspects of a candidate's previous behaviour, successes and skill gaps that are relevant to the job you are interviewing for.
- Don't make a job offer to any candidate if you have reservations about their ability to do the job well.

The lazy interviewer: ✕

- Fails to use a marking scheme
- Allows themselves to be swayed too easily during post-interview discussions
- Bases their decision on hunches and likeability rather than hard evidence
- Takes previous employer references at face value

The best interviewers: ✓

- Have a marking scheme in place before they see any candidates
- Base the marking scheme on the criteria they had chosen as most relevant to the job
- Are clear about the level of performance that equates to a pass, a fail or above-average markings
- Look carefully at the evidence they obtained at interview and use this as the basis for marking candidates
- Allocate marks intelligently
- Proactively engage with candidate's previous employers so as to get the most informative references possible

---

Coaches' Corner – Things for You to Try

- Try different types of marking schemes to suit different recruitment situations.
- Look at sample marking schemes from within your own company and elsewhere.
- Think about your own marking tendencies: are you an 'easy' or a 'hard' marker?

Postscript

When we started writing this book we expected it to be short and sweet – a summary of our experience as interviewers and trainers and a quick and sharp set of guidelines for anyone who faces having to interview or wrestles with the challenge of making the right selection. We were struck by just how much is involved in the process when we tried to squeeze it all between two covers. Hiring is a complex task, of that we have no doubt, but a focussed and planned approach and the application of those of our guidelines that will work for you should lead you to more certainty and more successful selections.

Interviewing is not a science, and you will never be 100 per cent certain that the decision you make is the right one until you see your new recruit in action, but it is worth the effort to get as close to that 100 per cent as possible. The rewards are obvious: getting someone who does the job well from day 1 is your ideal objective. You should aim to hire someone who will require the least training to bring them up to standard. If you hire someone with an obvious skill gap in the hope that coaching and training might help, you might never succeed in getting them to meet the demands of the job. If this happens you will be destined to spend more time and effort than you ever intended on the endless challenges associated with managing poor work performance.

When you make the right call there is a wholly different and positive experience for you and anyone else who has to work with the new recruit: the company derives the obvious benefits of having a productive and satisfied employee, and you gain a deep satisfaction in seeing the new recruit grow and develop over the years, knowing that you played a key role in their first steps on that journey to personal and career advancement.

We hope this book will be a positive influence on your quest to hire the right person, and we wish you all the best in that challenge.

Mary and *Brian*